# SHEIKH MOHAMMED

## LIFE AND TIMES

المكتب الإعلامي
لصاحب السمو الشيخ محمد بن راشد آل مكتوم

### THE MEDIA OFFICE
FOR H.H. SHEIKH MOHAMMED BIN RASHID AL MAKTOUM

# SHEIKH MOHAMMED

## LIFE AND TIMES

BY ROYAL PHOTOGRAPHER
NOOR ALI RASHID

MOTIVATE
PUBLISHING

# Dedication

*This book is respectfully dedicated to HH Sheikh Mohammed bin Rashid Al Maktoum, Vice-President and Prime Minister of the UAE and the Ruler of Dubai, for his vision, leadership and compassion.*
*— Noor Ali Rashid*

## Other Motivate titles by Noor Ali Rashid

*Abu Dhabi – Life & Times*
*Dubai – Life & Times*
*The UAE – Visions of Change*
*Sheikh Zayed – Life and Times*
*Sheikh Maktoum – Life and Times*
*Sheikh Khalifa – Life and Times*

## Published by Motivate Publishing

**Dubai**: PO Box 2331, Dubai, UAE
Tel: (+971 4) 282 4060, fax: (+971 4) 282 7898
e-mail: books@motivate.ae   www.booksarabia.com

Office 508, Building No 8, Dubai Media City, Dubai, UAE
Tel: (+971 4) 390 3550, fax: (+971 4) 390 4845

**Abu Dhabi**: PO Box 43072, Abu Dhabi, UAE
Tel: (+971 2) 677 2005, fax: (+971 2) 677 0124

**London**: Acre House, 11/15 William Road, London NW1 3ER
E-mail: motivateuk@motivate.ae

Directors:                          Obaid Humaid Al Tayer and Ian Fairservice
General Manager Books:  Jonathan Griffiths

Consultant Editor:        David Steele
Editors:                        Moushumi Nandy
                                   Simona Cassano
Senior Designer:           Cithadel Francisco
Designer:                     Charlie Banalo

Publishing Coordinator:   Zelda Pinto

## Other photographic credits
DIFC: 65
Dirk Laubner: 61
Dubai Metro: 66 (bottom)
Getty Images: 145
Gulfpics: 67 (top)
Jumeirah: 64
Nakheel: 67 (bottom)
Ronald Codrai © Justin Codrai: 16
The Media Office: 51, 59, 63 (top), 66 (top), 76 (top & bottom), 77, 79 (top & bottom), 80 (bottom right), 81, 82 (left), 84 (top & bottom), 85 (top & bottom), 86 (top & bottom), 87 (top & bottom), 88 (top right & top left), 89 (all), 91 (top & bottom), 96, 98, 99 (top & bottom), 100 (top & bottom), 101 (all), 116, 117, 118 (top), 120 (bottom), 121, 122, 123 (top & bottom), 124 (top & bottom), 125 (bottom), 131 (bottom), 137, 142 (bottom), 144
WAM/Emirates News Agency: 75, 78 (top), 80 (bottom left), 82 (top right and bottom right), 83 (top & bottom), 119, 136

## Author's Team
Photo Archivist: Shamsa Rashid
Photo Researcher: Samia Rashid
Editorial Coordinator: Yasmin Rashid

ISBN: 978 1 86063 202 0

British Library Cataloguing-in-Publication Data.
A catalogue record for this book is available from the British Library.

Printed and bound in the UAE by Emirates Printing Press, Dubai

*HH Sheikh Khalifa bin Zayed Al Nahyan*

Sheikh Mohammed's vision is an inseparable part of the government's comprehensive strategy, and we, as leaders, seek through its components to improve the living conditions of UAE citizens, upgrade education standards and provide all means of stability and strength to our country and citizens.

We all should be proud of this success as well as all other achievements of this great nation and its genuine Arab heritage, culture and values.


***Khalifa bin Zayed Al Nahyan***
*President of the UAE and Ruler of Abu Dhabi*
*April 15, 2009 on his visit to Dubai*

*HH Sheikh Mohammed bin Zayed Al Nahyan*

# Preface

It is with great pride that I introduce this book on His Highness Sheikh Mohammed bin Rashid Al Maktoum, Vice-President and Prime Minister of UAE and Ruler of Dubai. *Sheikh Mohammed – Life and Times* captivates the readers through words and pictures, and gives us a valuable insight into the most spectacular and luminous stations in the life of HH Sheikh Mohammed. Recording the accomplishments and hopes that sum up the life course of an entire nation, this brings to light the merits of the twenty-first century leader and statesman.

It seeks to highlight the leadership of Sheikh Mohammed in various economic, socio-cultural and human spheres, in addition to his integral role in developing the patriotic and political life of the UAE. This outstanding role combines the originality of the unique vision of his great father, the late Sheikh Rashid bin Saeed Al Maktoum, and his brother, the late Sheikh Maktoum bin Rashid Al Maktoum.

The vision of these three great leaders along with the immortal vision of the late Sheikh Zayed bin Sultan Al Nahyan, the founding President of the UAE has guided the country and given shape to its future, and continues to inspire the forthcoming generation in building a modern society, adhered to its long-established roots and rich traditions.

These institutional visions that distinguish the personality of HH Sheikh Mohammed bin Rashid Al Maktoum has provided the stimulus in creating a unique experience in the Emirate of Dubai – an experience that has bewildered the world. Dubai is now an exceptional place, combining both the latest human development and progress in various fields, yet rooted with immortal values of the past.

The brilliant success of Dubai and the other emirates has been accomplished under the enlightened and prudent leadership of the President of the UAE, His Highness Sheikh Khalifa bin Zayed Al Nahyan. This is clearly expressed by the vast humane dimension, which is based on the principles of dialogue, tolerance and diversity. These principles are a part of the exceptional vision of Sheikh Mohammed bin Rashid Al Maktoum, and simultaneously contribute to the consolidation of the interior and external policies of the country, rooted in the principles of uniting mankind. The great success of Dubai echoes throughout the Arab world and reflects the constructive efforts of Sheikh Mohammed in the Arab youth's advancement of education, culture and knowledge.

*Sheikh Mohammed – Life and Times* is well presented and makes an interesting read. Noor Ali's timeless photographs give us a vivid glimpse into the life and times of this great leader and will be a joy to readers everywhere.

***Mohammed bin Zayed Al Nahyan***
*Crown Prince of Abu Dhabi*
*Deputy Supreme Commander of the Armed Forces*

# Introduction

**HE Sheikh Nahayan Mabarak Al Nahayan**

His Highness Sheikh Mohammed bin Rashid Al Maktoum was cited recently by *Time* magazine as one of the world's most influential people. We in the United Arab Emirates have always realized His Highness Sheikh Mohammed's foresight and have enjoyed the benefits of his enlightened leadership. We are greatly inspired by his vision for Dubai and the UAE and we are proud of his tireless work for peace and prosperity in Dubai, the UAE, and the world.

I am very pleased to write this introduction to this pictorial record of the life and achievements of Sheikh Mohammed. *Sheikh Mohammed – Life and Times* is a most welcome addition to the literature about Sheikh Mohammed bin Rashid. Readers will enjoy this opportunity to observe glimpses of a life that has helped shape our country and our region.

Sheikh Mohammed's dynamic and historic leadership has helped the UAE emerge as an important and integral part of the global economy. Under the leadership of our President, His Highness Sheikh Khalifa bin Zayed Al Nahyan, and with the strong support of His Highness Sheikh Mohammed bin Rashid Al Maktoum, the UAE is a country of peace, hope, opportunity and prosperity. It plays a prominent role in regional and international affairs. The UAE embodies tolerance and cooperation. We emphasize the importance of maintaining peace and stability in the region and around the world so that international cooperation can flourish and free trade and investment can thrive.

I am particularly appreciative of Sheikh Mohammed's emphasis on the creation of a knowledge economy in the United Arab Emirates. I admire his strong conviction that this economy depends directly upon a highly educated society. We are very fortunate to have Sheikh

Mohammed's strong support for education. We value his absolute belief that both men and women should have equal educational opportunities, and that every citizen possesses the right to develop their God-given talents to the fullest. Sheikh Mohammed's vision for the future also includes other critical aspects of human development: innovation, health, social welfare, charitable work, safety and security. He focuses great attention on these areas in his role as the Vice-President and the Prime Minister of the United Arab Emirates.

Sheikh Mohammed is a change maker who is rarely satisfied with the status quo. He is a remarkable leader with a remarkable record of achievement. He is a leader of many fronts – a statesman, an economist, a poet, and a sportsman. He motivates and influences all of us, setting high expectations for our individual and collective endeavours. Leading visibly and by example, he accepts responsibility and does not shy from difficult and necessary decisions. Sheikh Mohammed shows tremendous skill for team building and he does not hesitate to seek input from others.

Sheikh Mohammed's ground-breaking book, *My Vision – Challenges in the Race for Excellence*, is heralded by reviewers as one of the most important books published in the middle East in the past 50 years. This remarkable book describes and explains the values and principles of effective leadership that have led to the tremendous success of Dubai. The book clearly reflects Sheikh Mohammed's great pride in his heritage and his identity, as well as his confidence in the UAE, its people, and its leadership.

I am proud to have this opportunity to express my greatest respect and admiration for His Highness Sheikh Mohammed bin Rashid Al Maktoum. His intellectual capacity, his imaginative vision, his courage and conviction, and his ability to transform vision into reality are sources of great pride to all of us in the United Arab Emirates.

A historic personality, Sheikh Mohammed leads a full, fascinating, and rewarding life. In *Sheikh Mohammed – Life and Times*, the author, Noor Ali Rashid has captured some very interesting aspects of this life. This collection of extraordinary photographs demonstrates how the leadership of Sheikh Mohammed builds and transforms our society. I am confident that this book will be received with great interest by readers everywhere.

**Sheikh Nahayan Mabarak Al Nahayan**
*Minister of Higher Education and Scientific Research*
*United Arab Emirates*

# Contents

Dubai Creek has played a pivotal role in the history of the emirate, with the natural anchorage providing a rare haven on the trade routes that ran through the Gulf, linking Africa and the Far East. Even today, the Creek remains the heart and soul of the city.

# Chapter 1

# The early years 1948–1968

**The start of the Al Maktoum dynasty**

Historians point to 1833 as the start of Dubai's modern history. That year, some 800 members of the Al Bu Falasah branch of the Bani Yas tribe left Abu Dhabi for Dubai, where they settled along the banks of its Creek. They made their living from fishing, trade and pearl diving and were led by Ubaid bin Saeed and Maktoum bin Buti Al Maktoum until the death of the former in 1836, leaving Sheikh Maktoum in sole power. This was the start of the dynamic royal dynasty that established a strong and prosperous emirate and has ruled the emirate ever since.

The settlement of the Al Bu Falasah branch in Dubai came soon after another branch of the Bani Yas tribal confederation moved from the Liwa Oasis, on the edge of the Rub al-Khali[1] or Empty Quarter, one of the world's largest sand deserts, to the island of Abu Dhabi. Their move to Abu Dhabi marked the start of another enduring royal dynasty – that of the Al Nahyan family – which still rules Abu Dhabi today and has provided the UAE with its first two presidents, the late Sheikh Zayed and his son Sheikh Khalifa.

Under the rule of Sheikh Maktoum, the Al Bu Falasah quickly turned to pearl diving, a lucrative, albeit dangerous endeavour that played a vital role in outlining the future of Dubai as a prominent regional trade centre, thanks to its geographical proximity to India, Iran and other Gulf countries. Secondary industries such as boat and shipbuilding thrived alongside pearl trading and other goods, providing employment for most of the area's young men. Trade routes grew, with the neighbouring Iranian Lingah port providing the first outlet for Dubai's coveted natural pearls. Indian businessmen, mostly from Bombay, arrived to capitalize on Dubai's growth while the emirate's Rulers invested the proceeds of the custom duties, levied on imported goods, to gradually develop and bring

---

[1] The Rub al-Khali covers 650,000 square kilometres and encompasses most of the southern part of the Arabian Peninsula, including southern Saudi Arabia and large parts of Oman and the UAE.

security and stability, thus further promoting its prosperity.

Any hope for sustained commercial progress was dashed when the combined effects of the First World War, the worldwide Great Depression, the Second World War and the introduction of cultured pearl by the Japanese in the 1930s took their toll. Dubai's flourishing pearl industry also suffered a mortal blow during this period. Nevertheless the emirate, with its thriving port, well-established souk and trading infrastructure, was better placed than a number of other Gulf towns. Much of this diversification was a result of the efforts of Sheikh Mohammed's grandfather, Sheikh Saeed bin Maktoum Al Maktoum, who ruled the emirate for 46 years from 1912 until his death in 1958 and established the foundations of Dubai as we know it today.

Sheikh Saeed was succeeded by his first-born son, the late Sheikh Rashid bin Saeed Al Maktoum, who ruled with extraordinary vision for 32 years from 1958 until 1990. It is notable that between father and son, Dubai enjoyed 78 years of remarkable stability and progress in a century that was regarded elsewhere as unstable and hostile.

Oil was discovered at the offshore Fateh Field in 1966 and production started in 1969. Soon thereafter Sheikh Rashid, with his usual futuristic vision, realized that Dubai's oil would soon run out and decided to invest its revenues in developing a sustainable and diversified economy that can still thrive long after the depletion of the oil wealth.

Reflecting on this, Sheikh Rashid used to say:

> My grandfather rode a camel, my father rode a camel, I drive a Mercedes, my son and his son and their offspring will drive Land Rovers, but my great grandson might be forced to ride camels again, if we don't do anything to sustain our prosperous economy.

Sheikh Rashid was right. In 2006, oil and natural gas revenues accounted for only three per cent of Dubai's

---

RIGHT: **A rare portrait of Sheikh Mohammed in his early teens.**

TOP: Sheikh Mohammed (second to the left) and Sheikh Maktoum bin Rashid Al Maktoum (extreme right), inaugurating the Pepsi Cola bottling plant in Dubai. Also seen in the picture (from right to left) are, Ahmed Al Ghurair, Mohammed Al Qaz and Mehdi Al Tajer.

ABOVE: A young, intent-looking Sheikh Mohammed with his oldest brother, Sheikh Maktoum.

LEFT: Sheikh Mohammed reading a book with his father, Sheikh Rashid bin Saeed Al Maktoum.

Dhs 170 billion GDP. Sheikh Rashid's vision was to transform Dubai into a modern city, enjoying a dynamic, open and diversified economy, attracting investments and trade from all over the world by launching a multipronged series of bold and ambitious utilities, infrastructure, services and manufacturing projects, something that many considered as mere beautiful dreams that will never become a reality.

Soon after, however, those dreams and projects, contested by so many, became true and established their feasibility and viability. Examples of those far-sighted projects include the dredging of the Dubai Creek and the construction of the Al Maktoum Bridge, Port Rashid, Al Maktoum Hospital[2], Dubai Airport, Dubai World Trade Centre[3], Jebel Ali Port, Jebel Ali Free Zone and the Dubai Aluminium Company (Dubal).

Perhaps the most impressive of all the legacies of Sheikh Rashid, was that his faithful sons were well educated, groomed in government affairs and ready to continue his good work after he departed. Dubai prospered under the rule of the late Sheikh Maktoum bin Rashid Al Maktoum, who became Ruler in 1990 and was ably assisted by his brethren to lead the emirate to further prosperity and successes.

Motivated as always by the need to reaffirm continuity and constancy, Sheikh Maktoum bin Rashid Al Maktoum decided to appoint Sheikh Mohammed bin Rashid Al Maktoum as Crown Prince on January 4, 1995, and appointed His Highness Sheikh Hamdan bin Rashid Al Maktoum as Deputy Ruler.

Following soon after the death of the former President of the United Arab Emirates and Ruler of Abu Dhabi, Sheikh Zayed bin Sultan Al Nahyan, on November 2, 2004, the sudden, unexpected death of the former Vice-President and Prime Minister of the UAE and Ruler of Dubai, the Sheikh Maktoum bin Rashid Al Maktoum, in Australia on January 4, 2006, was a huge shock to his admirers in Dubai and the other emirates of the UAE. In little more than two years, the Emirates had lost two much loved leaders. There had been nothing quite like it since the death of Sheikh Rashid bin Saeed Al Maktoum, the first Vice-President, Prime Minister of the UAE and Ruler of Dubai, in 1990.

Meeting on January 5, 2006, the UAE Supreme Council of Rulers unanimously approved the appointment of His Highness Sheikh Mohammed bin Rashid Al Maktoum as

---

[2] The first modern hospital to be established in the Trucial States that today constitute the United Arab Emirates.

[3] Previously known as the Trade Centre, it is still one of Dubai's prominent landmarks and was at the time the tallest building in the Middle East.

ABOVE: Quite understandably, many of Dubai's administrative buildings were situated along the banks of the Creek. Originally built as a residence and a *diwan* (Ruler's Office) for Sheikh Saeed in 1954 when he moved from Sheikh Saeed House in Shindagha, the building in the foreground later housed the Customs Office, warehouses and a primary school. Al Fahidi Fort and the Friday Mosque are also visible in this photograph.

LEFT: An aerial view of the Bastakiya area with its windtower houses and the old custom house on the banks of the Creek. Today, the *diwan* is situated in the area to the left.

Vice-President and Prime Minister of the UAE, following his earlier appointment as the Ruler of Dubai, making him the best successor of a great predecessor. His Highness Sheikh Mohammed bin Rashid Al Maktoum also retained his post as the UAE's Minister of Defence.

While the deaths of Sheikh Zayed and Sheikh Maktoum came as a huge shock, Sheikh Mohammed's rise to power was not at all surprising. After all, his father, Sheikh Rashid bin Saeed Al Maktoum, had been grooming him for a position of power since he was little more than a boy. Sheikh Mohammed is the tenth Ruler of Dubai and the tenth Ruler of the Maktoum dynasty.

**Born to rule**
Sheikh Mohammed was born in 1949, the third of Sheikh Rashid and his wife Sheikha Latifa bint Hamdan Al Nahyan's four sons. He enjoyed a happy and carefree childhood at his family home in Shindagha where his parents and grandfather, Sheikh Saeed, lavished affection on him. His playmates were his brothers, cousins and the children of Dubai's major trading families.

Time spent alongside his grandfather in his Shindagha *majlis* exposed the young sheikh to Arab folktales and poetry that would become intrinsic to his later life. The experience also afforded him the opportunity to listen to discussions on current issues, an invaluable form of early education that invariably moulded his strong and open leadership style, based on listening to people's aspirations and accommodating them.

Early on he was taught hunting and falconry and finds the latter sport "an opportunity to return to his Arab roots and distance himself from the pace of modern world". Sheikh Rashid also taught Sheikh Mohammed bin Rashid Al Maktoum the rudiments of horsemanship and the young Sheikh Mohammed and his friends could soon be seen riding every day. He began his studies at the tender age of four before enrolling at Al Ahmedia School, a small primary school in Deira, the creekside area that had fostered the town's early settlement and industry. He studied Arabic, English, mathematics, geography and history before moving on to Al Shaab School at the age of 10. Two years later he joined the Dubai Secondary School. A keen student with a photographic memory, Sheikh Mohammed progressed through the academic phases of his schooling with ease.

When Sheikh Saeed passed away in 1958, Sheikh Rashid became the Ruler and immediately began making preparations for his sons' future involvement in governing Dubai. Despite his youth, Sheikh Mohammed bin Rashid Al Maktoum was one of Sheikh Rashid's inner circle of talented individuals and had become a valuable participant in the discussions.

From the outset, Sheikh Rashid earmarked his son His Highness Sheikh Mohammed as someone whose talents would be best suited in managing Dubai's increasing security demands. However, before he received any military training, he needed to become proficient in the English language. In August 1966, Sheikh Mohammed bin Rashid Al Maktoum and his cousin Sheikh Mohammed bin Khalifa Al Maktoum flew to London and enrolled in the Bell School of Languages in Cambridge, a melting pot of nationalities and cultures.

In 1967, Sheikh Mohammed joined the Mons Officer Cadet School at Aldershot, about 65 kilometres from London. Aldershot was home to the British Army's first Corps and the staging point from which troops left for both the First and Second World Wars. Following in the footsteps of the academy's most-famous graduate, Sir Winston Churchill, Prime Minister of Great Britain during the Second World War, His Highness studied civil and military aviation. He quickly rose to the challenge of his new surroundings, adapting to the demands of six months of intense military training and study. During the latter stages of his course he was promoted to Chief Warrant Officer and was later awarded the Sword of Honour for achieving the highest mark of any foreign and Commonwealth officer cadet in his intake.

Aldershot attracted students from across the globe and, once again exposed His Highness Sheikh Mohammed bin Rashid Al Maktoum to a wide variety of cultures. This experience no doubt affected the leader whose homeland welcomes citizens of all nationalities to live and work in the UAE and enjoy the dignified lifestyle it offers them.

When Sheikh Mohammed returned to Dubai in 1968, following his graduation, he had a very good understanding of the areas that would be of importance in his adult life: military, politics, literature, sports and, perhaps most importantly, the art of leadership.

RIGHT: This aerial photograph of Dubai Creek dates back to the 1960s. The Al Ahmedia School, which Sheikh Mohammed attended, has now been renovated as a tourist attraction and is visible at the centre of the picture, along the bend of the Creek.

Dubai and the region's old souks relied heavily on primitive local products in meeting the needs of the local populations. The picture at the top, on the opposite page shows a retailer displaying his goods, including rosaries, pottery and canes, while the picture below shows a group of women selling household goods, such as small cheese balls, large thin tortilla-like bread, cottage butter 'ghee', *kohl* powder and assorted cosmetics and herbal medicines. Seen on this page is a retailer selling assorted goods.

LEFT TOP: In olden times, Dubai's residents relied on fishing and pearl diving for their subsistence, but the Creek dredging project introduced deep changes to the emirate's economy. Seen here are *gargours* (fish traps) piled high aboard dhows bound for the fishing grounds.

LEFT BOTTOM: An aerial photograph of the Dubai Creek dating back to the 1960s, which clearly shows the three distinct 'communities' which then made up Dubai. Shindagha in the left foreground, Bur Dubai (including Bastakiya) to the right, and Deira on the far side of the Creek.

ABOVE: The Clock Tower was one of the first modern structures to appear in Dubai. Today it is surrounded by hotel apartments and modern buildings.

OPPOSITE PAGE, TOP: Bastakiya in the late 1960s. The area has been renovated and is now preserved as a cultural district.

OPPOSITE PAGE, BOTTOM: This image shows some of the first tarred roads in Dubai. The Fikhri Building seen here has been renovated and is now one of Dubai's heritage buildings.

Al Maktoum Bridge, which was inaugurated by Sheikh Rashid, was the first bridge to be built in the emirate, to ease traffic between Deira and Bur Dubai without having to use the *abra*. The bridge enabled goods to move quickly from Customs Wharves at Bur Dubai to the Deira Dhow Wharves where these goods were traded and shipped to neighbouring Gulf countries.

The construction of the Dubai airport was one of the emirate's major development projects.
Ever since its inauguration, the airport witnessed a flurry of upgrading and expansion projects.

ABOVE AND OPPOSITE PAGE, TOP: Seen in these two images are large crowds of citizens and
expatriates gathering at the airport's terminal to greet Sheikh Rashid bin Saeed Al
Maktoum upon his return from an overseas trip.

OPPOSITE PAGE, BOTTOM: The new terminal, named after Sheikh Rashid, was officially opened in
1971, providing evidence of the growth of air traffic between Dubai and distant destinations.

# *Chapter 2*

# A royal apprenticeship: 1968–1995

The future of His Highness Sheikh Mohammed bin Rashid Al Maktoum was revealed to him at an early age. His father, Sheikh Rashid bin Saeed Al Maktoum had begun to prepare his sons to handle government affairs since their early teens, a domain Sheikh Mohammed excelled at. His Highness was always very keen on keeping his father and grandfather company, which allowed him to polish his leadership skills at an early age. His days at the UK's Cambridge College and the Aldershot Military College rounded off his formal education.

In February 1968, Sheikh Zayed bin Sultan Al Nahyan and Sheikh Rashid bin Saeed Al Maktoum met at a desert campsite to discuss a federation between the two emirates Abu Dhabi and Dubai. Sheikh Mohammed flew back from London especially to accompany his father to this crucial meeting and still remembers the brief discussion between the two leaders that later led to the establishment of the United Arab Emirates. Sheikh Zayed then asked Sheikh Rashid: "What do you think Rashid? Should we establish a federation?" Instantaneously, Sheikh Rashid held out his hand forward and said: "Put your hand forward O' Zayed, so that I can shake hands with you to confirm a done deal, and you shall be the President".

Their historic agreement, known as the Union Accord, was the beginning of an initiative for a wider federation, involving Ajman, Fujairah, Ra's al-Khaimah, Sharjah and Umm al-Qaiwain. Bahrain and Qatar were also involved in the discussions.

Sheikh Zayed, Sheikh Rashid and their sons, including His Highness Sheikh Mohammed bin Rashid Al Maktoum, strived for the success of these talks that took some four years. The talks were crowned by the establishment of the United Arab Emirates on December 2, 1971. In the end, Bahrain and Qatar never joined the federation and Ra's al-Khaimah joined the six other emirates early in 1972.

**Military beginnings**
A short while after the 1968 historic meeting between the two great leaders Sheikh Zayed and Sheikh Rashid, His Highness Sheikh Mohammed bin Rashid Al Maktoum

returned to the UAE, eager to put all the leadership and military skills he acquired overseas at the service of his homeland. In November 1968, only months after he had graduated from Aldershot, Sheikh Rashid appointed Sheikh Mohammed as Head of Dubai Police and Public Security. This was Sheikh Mohammed's first public position and one in which he excelled.

Three years after the establishment of the federation, Sheikh Maktoum bin Rashid Al Maktoum, then the country's new Prime Minister, appointed his brother, Sheikh Mohammed to the post of Minister of Defence – a position he still holds today – and promoted him to the rank of General and Commander of the UAE Army. The appointment made history, as Sheikh Mohammed was the youngest Minister of Defence at the time, but he quickly proved himself worthy of the challenge and the huge responsibilities of his new post.

His Highness didn't have long to enjoy this extraordinary acclaim before he was called into action to deal with the repercussions of an Arab-Israeli war, a coup in a neighbouring country and hijacking incidents involving Dubai International Airport in 1972 and 1973.

With the integration of the various defence forces of the different emirates into a single national force, the Union Defence Force became the Federal Armed Forces in 1974 and the UAE Armed Forces in 1976. Throughout his military career, Sheikh Mohammed faced difficult decisions, including the choice to commit his newly trained troops to assist the Arab Deterrent Force during Lebanon's 1976 civil war, where the UAE troops served

---

RIGHT: Sheikh Mohammed was appointed Head of Dubai Police and Security in 1968 and UAE Minister of Defence after federation in 1971, following the establishment of the UAE, to become the youngest Minister of Defence in the world at the time.

FOLLOWING SPREAD: The Dubai International Trade Centre (now known as the Dubai World Trade Centre) was completed in 1979. The long modern road running in front of the building is Sheikh Zayed Road.

until 1979. His Highness always showed strong leadership skills and singularity of vision in dealing with these matters.

Sheikh Rashid granted his sons substantial powers to realize his dream of transforming Dubai into a modern, prosperous and advanced emirate. In almost constant counsel with one another, especially throughout their lives as public figures, his sons formed a united front. Sheikh Mohammed bin Rashid Al Maktoum, Sheikh Hamdan bin Rashid Al Maktoum and Sheikh Maktoum bin Rashid Al Maktoum conferred daily and shared whatever information they had about public and state affairs and adopting resolutions.

Ever since his early youth, Sheikh Mohammed played a crucial role in fulfilling the dream of his father, because of his unique ability to take difficult resolutions in a clear, confident and determined way. His Highness acquired substantial experience by constantly accompanying Sheikh Rashid, whom he resembled so much in his daily life, to the point that many likened Sheikh Mohammed's own *majlis* to that of his late father. "It is a creative environment in which people are allowed to speak freely," explained local businessman Mohammed Al Naboodah.

> Sheikh Mohammed put no barriers on what can be said, because His Highness believed that only such a kind of open debate can lead to fruitful results. His Highness used to challenge people to think and perform beyond what they assumed were their limit, because this is the only way to bring out the best in people.

**Mega projects**

In the 1970s and 1980s Dubai witnessed a flurry of mega infrastructure, industrial, services and construction projects that laid the foundations for its now prosperous economy. The Dubai Drydocks, the biggest facility of its kind in the Middle East was one of the first mega projects His Highness Sheikh Mohammed bin Rashid Al Maktoum was assigned to supervise and follow through their implementation, in addition to the oil industry. In 1977, His Highness was assigned the presidency of a committee formed to take over the administration of Dubai International Airport.

The year 1979 is an especially significant year in Dubai's history as it witnessed the completion and inauguration of three of the emirate's largest projects. The first of these was the port of Jebel Ali. The second was the aluminium smelter, constructed and owned by Dubai Aluminium Company (Dubal), with an initial annual capacity of 135,000 tonnes. The third mega project commissioned that year was the Dubai International Trade Centre (now known as the Dubai World Trade Centre), the tallest building in the Middle East

ABOVE: From a young age, Sheikh Mohammed and his brothers were groomed by their father to assume future leadership positions.

LEFT: Sheikh Mohammed waiting to bid his father, Sheikh Rashid bin Saeed Al Maktoum, farewell at the Dubai Airport. Also seen here is Ahmed bin Sulayem (second from right), a great friend of Sheikh Rashid.

at the time and one of the world's tallest today. Recalling his memories of those glorious days, Sheikh Mohammed said:

From the outset, my father the late Sheikh Rashid bin Saeed Al Maktoum, was keen on providing Dubai with a sophisticated and unique infrastructure and a successful industrial base that transformed the emirate into a prominent regional business centre, at an early stage of its development.

He continued to build upon his father's dream when Sheikh Rashid fell ill in 1981, and ordered the Jebel Ali Port to be expanded to include the Jebel Ali Free Zone (JAFZA) in 1985. The move further promoted Dubai's reputation as a fully fledged, huge international and integral shipping, warehousing, distribution, trade and manufacturing centre. Today, JAFZA boasts more than 5,000 companies, active in all fields and constantly expanding and providing a major boost to Dubai's GDP.

Recalling the early leadership and follow up of Dubai's development by His Highness Sheikh Mohammed, a senior official said:

One of the main points His Highness emphasized was the need to keep things simple. He worked to ensure JAFZA was served by the best in infrastructure that would empower it to offer the best services possible.

Establishing Emirates Airline to jumpstart Dubai's aviation and tourism industries was one of Sheikh Mohammed's ambitious development ventures. In January 1985, Maurice Flanagan, then General Manager of the Dubai National Tourism Authority (DNATA), was summoned to Sheikh Mohammed's Za'abeel Palace. "I want to start an airline as soon as possible. How much will it cost? And how long will it take?", His Highness asked. "Ten million dollars," responded Flanagan, knowing well that

ABOVE: Sheikh Rashid and his entourage inspect the Margham Field, the first onshore oil rig in Dubai. Seen from right to left are: His Highness Sheikh Mohammed, Abdul Kareem Taqizadeh (who was also known as Captain and was a keen photographer), an oil company executive, His Highness Sheikh Rashid, Mehdi Al Tajer, Salem Musabah, Humaid Al Tayer, Sheikh Omar bin Obaid Al Majid and their helicopter pilot.

LEFT: Sheikh Mohammed aboard a helicopter during an inspection of Dubai's oil fields.

His Highness was not a man who would wait around for an answer.

Sheikh Mohammed set up a small team to develop the project, and on October 25 that year Emirates took its maiden flight sporting livery chosen by His Highness Sheikh Mohammed personally. Since its launch, and despite rising fuel costs that put several other airlines out of business, Emirates has achieved unprecedented levels of success, ordering dozens of Airbus and Boeing aircraft in hefty multi-billion-dollar deals. Dubai's open skies policy and present position as a world aviation and tourism hub is considered to be one of Sheikh Mohammed's greatest achievements.

Despite Middle Eastern crises such as Lebanon's invasion, the Iran-Iraq War and the beginning of the Palestinian Intifada on December 9, 1987, Sheikh Mohammed continued to support Dubai's quick paced development.

"There was a self-belief within the Dubai and Federal Government," explained Financial Analyst Clinton Jones:

> The Maktoum brothers in particular were not content to tread water and wait until stability returned. Indeed, there was a trend regionally to increase holdings in Europe and North America. Dubai bucked this trend. To boost local economy, there was greater spending on infrastructural projects. In doing so, Dubai showed its overwhelming confidence in itself and the future. This helped to calm the Dubai economy and laid the foundations for the bright future we see today.

Just as everything in Dubai seemed to be proceeding well, a dark cloud cast its shadow over the blossoming country on an October morning in 1990. Nine years after he first fell ill, Sheikh Rashid bin Saeed Al Maktoum, the beloved 'Father of Dubai', died. Sheikh Maktoum bin Rashid Al Maktoum assumed the post of Ruler of Dubai and was named UAE Vice-President and Prime Minister shortly after.

**A busy time for the Minister of Defence**

Sheikh Rashid bin Saeed Al Maktoum's legacy had gained such strong momentum that there was little time for his sons to grieve and dwell upon their loss before having to shift their focus to a national crisis. Iraq had launched an invasion into Kuwait only weeks earlier. All capable national men were ordered to join the armed forces for six weeks of mandatory military training and the UAE Armed Forces, together with forces from other GCC states, participated in the liberation of Kuwait as part of the International Alliance.

The UAE Armed Forces took part in Operation Desert Shield from August 1990 to February 1991 and Operation

ABOVE: **As soon as he became Ruler of Dubai, Sheikh Rashid bin Saeed Al Maktoum began to prepare his sons to shoulder the responsibilities of their emirate and assigned Sheikh Mohammed the responsibility of the oil industry. His Highness is seen here checking an off-shore oil rig, accompanied by Sheikh Saqr bin Sultan Al Qasimi. Whenever Sheikh Rashid bin Saeed Al Maktoum sent Sheikh Mohammed on an important assignment, he would also send Noor Ali Rashid to cover the same event.**

RIGHT: **From left to right: His Highness Sheikh Mohammed bin Rashid Al Maktoum accompanying his father Sheikh Rashid bin Saeed Al Maktoum on a tour of one of Dubai's oil fields. Also seen in the picture is Mehdi Al Tajer (the former ambassador to the UK) and Humaid Al Tayer.**

Desert Storm in February 1991. The UAE Air Force was also actively involved from the beginning of operations, and flew 173 sorties with no losses. In capturing 1,203 enemy officers and soldiers, as well as a large number of weapons, the ground forces lost 10 men and 15 of them were wounded.

On March 4, 1991, Sheikh Mohammed issued a statement to mark the UAE's first involvement in war:

> The UAE's armed forces were at the forefront of coalition efforts to liberate Kuwait. We have been made extremely proud by your bravery and commitment to the cause of justice. Many of my peers from other countries called me to praise the role played by our valiant armed forces. The United Arab Emirates will continue to stand for peace, steadfast in its support of its friends. The Emirates remain a cosmopolitan oasis, where differing cultures and religions coexist in peace. It is this model of tolerance that we hope to export to the rest of the world.

His Highness Sheikh Mohammed bin Rashid Al Maktoum called for an international force to be sent to Bosnia to counter the Serbian aggression, making it clear that the UAE would be willing to participate. When the UN mission in

Bosnia and Herzegovina was eventually created it came under NATO command. Since the UAE was not a member of the alliance, it did not participate directly, although the Ministry of Defence provided numerous airlifts of wounded Bosnian Muslims to Abu Dhabi and Dubai for medical treatment. Their accompanying families were given accommodation and financial support. At the same time, many UAE leaders, including Sheikh Mohammed, generously donated money to support the Bosnians during the conflict and helped rebuild Bosnia once peace was restored.

Back home, in January 1993, His Highness was able to play a more active role in another crisis, this time in Africa. A famine in war-devastated Somalia had been compounded by internal strife, and the UAE, under directives from the Sheikh Zayed, dispatched a task force to the country from January 1993 to April 1994. In addition to controlling two Somali areas and securing Mogadishu Harbour, the force undertook several vital humanitarian tasks.

Against this background, in a surprise double-decree on January 3, 1995, Sheikh Maktoum bin Rashid Al Maktoum, then Ruler of Dubai, named His Highness Sheikh Mohammed bin Rashid Al Maktoum as Crown Prince, just prior to his fiftieth birthday, and named His Highness Sheikh Hamdan bin Rashid Al Maktoum, the Minister of Finance, as Deputy Ruler of Dubai.

A new era had begun in the UAE's history.

ABOVE: Sheikh Rashid relied increasingly on his sons as he sought to transform Dubai, and in addition to becoming the world's youngest Minister of Defence, Sheikh Mohammed was in charge of projects such as the Dubai Drydocks and the Dubai International Airport.

LEFT: During the 1970s Sheikh Mohammed was assigned the responsibility of supervising Dubai's oil industry, then one of the most vital tasks within the Dubai Government. Here he is seen before travelling by helicopter to one of the rigs.

RIGHT: Sheikh Mohammed took a keen interest in the public affairs of Dubai and the other emirates.

OPPOSITE PAGE, TOP: Sheikh Rashid is seen on the right of the photo, at Dubai Airport, with Sheikh Mohammed and Sheikh Maktoum in the centre.

BOTTOM: Sheikh Mohammed (second from right), attending one of the meetings of the Government of Dubai, presided by his father Sheikh Rashid bin Saeed Al Maktoum, and his brother Sheikh Maktoum bin Rashid Al Maktoum. Also seen in the picture is Adi Bitar, the legal adviser to the Ruler's office and Kamal Hamza, the Ex-Director General of Dubai Municipality.

There were those who forecast that a federation between the seven emirates would never work. Perhaps these prophets of doom undervalued the enduring relationships that existed between the ruling families of the different emirates and how today's rulers would strengthen the bonds forged by their fathers.

Above: His Highness Sheikh Mohammed with His Highness Sheikh Hamad bin Mohammed Al Sharqi, the present Ruler of Fujairah.

Opposite page, top: Sheikh Mohammed with Sheikh Mubarak bin Mohammed Al Nahyan, the former Minister of Interior.

Opposite page, bottom: Sheikh Mohammed (centre) with Sheikh Rashid bin Ahmed Al Mualla, Ruler of Umm al-Qaiwain, in conversation with Sheikh Saqr bin Sultan Al Qasimi, the Ruler of Ra's al-Khaimah.

ABOVE: Sheikh Mohammed takes the oath of a Federal Minister in the presence of Sheikh Zayed and Sheikh Maktoum during the creation of the first Government of the United Arab Emirates.

OPPOSITE PAGE, TOP: Sheikh Mohammed bin Rashid (centre), at the signing ceremony of the convention establishing the United Arab Emirates. Seen in the picture from the left are: Sheikh Rashid, Sheikh Maktoum, Sheikh Hamdan, Sheikh Mohammed bin Sultan Al Qasimi, and Sheikh Khalid bin Mohammed Al Qasimi.

OPPOSITE PAGE, BOTTOM: Sheikh Mohammed and Sheikh Maktoum at the Union House in Dubai, following one of the federation meetings for establishing the United Arab Emirates. Also seen in the picture is Sheikh Saif bin Mohammed Al Nahyan (centre).

FOLLOWING SPREAD: Two pictures separated by 38 years. To the left, Sheikh Zayed bin Sultan Al Nahyan and Sheikh Rashid bin Saeed Al Maktoum, attending the raising ceremony of the United Arab Emirates' flag for the first time on December 2, 1971. The ceremony was also attended by their Highnesses the Rulers and a huge crowd of citizens and expatriates. His Highness Sheikh Mohammed bin Rashid Al Maktoum is seen to the left of the picture. Also seen here is the late Sheikh Khalid bin Mohammed Al Qasimi, the then Ruler of Sharjah and Sheikh Mohammed bin Hamad Al Sharqi, the then Ruler of Fujairah. The flag was raised at the Union House in Dubai, a part of which is seen in the picture's background, and which used to be the guest house of Sheikh Rashid bin Saeed Al Maktoum before becoming the seat of the negotiations for establishing the United Arab Emirates. To the left, we see His Highness Sheikh Khalifa bin Zayed, the President of the UAE and the Supreme Commander of the Armed Forces, touring a number of Dubai's gigantic projects, thus promoting the true spirit of the Union, accompanied by His Highness Sheikh Mohammed bin Rashid Al Maktoum, Vice-President and Prime Minister of the UAE and Ruler of Dubai; His Highness General Sheikh Mohammed bin Zayed Al Nahyan, Crown Prince of Abu Dhabi and Deputy Supreme Commander of the Armed Forces and His Highness Sheikh Mansour bin Zayed Al Nahyan, Deputy Prime Minister and Minister of Presidential Affairs on his right. To his left are, His Highness Sheikh Tahnoun bin Mohammed Al Nahyan, the Representative of the Ruler of Abu Dhabi in the Eastern Region; His Highness Sheikh Hazza bin Zayed Al Nahyan, National Security Adviser of the UAE and His Highness Sheikh Mohammed bin Khalifa Al Nahyan, Chairman of Abu Dhabi's Department of Finance.

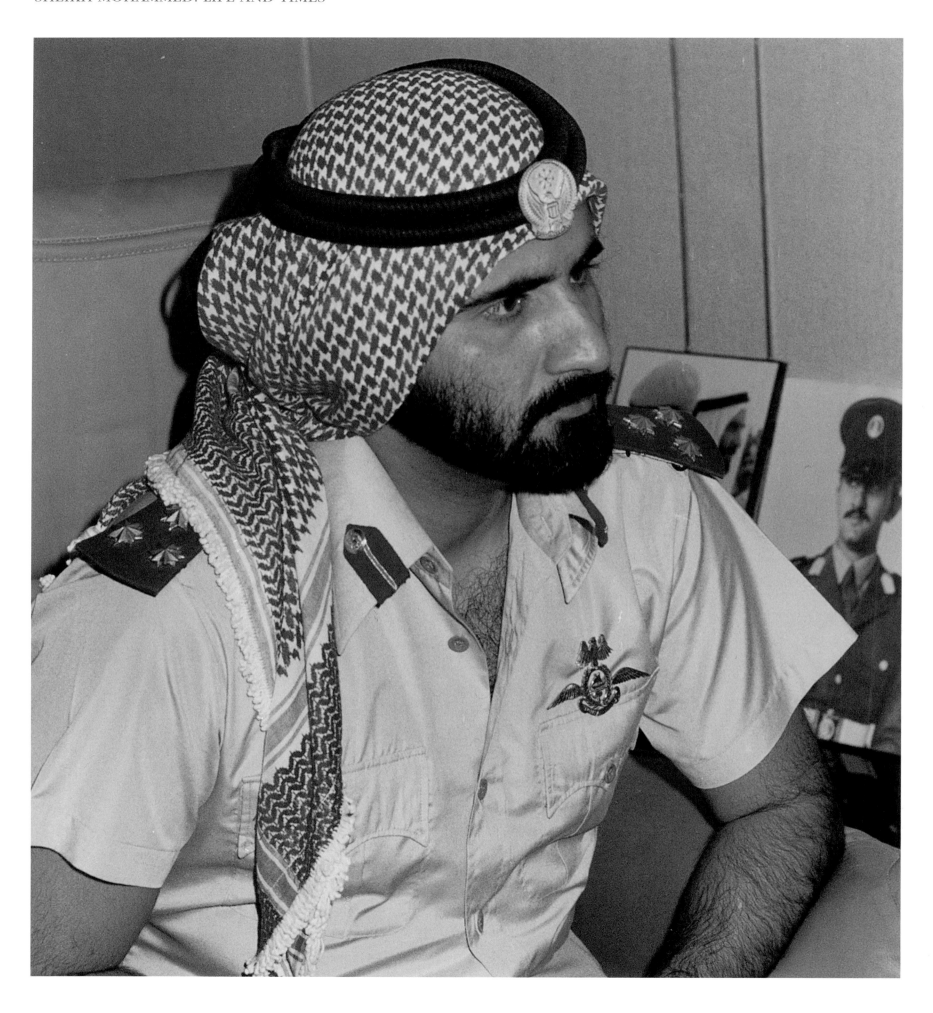

In 1968, Sheikh Rashid appointed Sheikh Mohammed as Head of Dubai
Police and Public Security. After federation three years later, Sheikh
Mohammed's brother, the country's new Prime Minister, Sheikh
Maktoum, appointed him to the post of Minister of Defence and
promoted him to the rank of General and Commander of the UAE Army.

ABOVE: A charming portrait of Sheikh Mohammed as a young man.

RIGHT: Sheikh Mohammed made full use of his visits to other countries to develop his vision for Dubai. Here he is seen in the cockpit of a fighter plane exhibited at Farnborough, UK.

The Trucial States and the United Kingdom have enjoyed close bonds since 1820 and agreed to a Perpetual Maritime Truce in 1853 (giving rise to the names 'Trucial Sheikhdoms' and 'Trucial States'). In 1968 the UK announced its decision to withdraw from the Gulf by the end of 1971 – a decision which led to federation and the formation of the UAE on December 2, 1971. The two countries have retained strong ties and a warm and friendly relationship since federation, and members of the British Royal Family and British parliamentarians continue to pay regular visits to the UAE and Dubai.

ABOVE: His Highness Sheikh Mohammed receiving the British Conservative leader, Edward Heath, who toured the Gulf in 1968 to assess the local reaction to the British withdrawal from the Trucial States planned by the Labour Government.

OPPOSITE PAGE, TOP: The Princess Royal, Princess Ann, meets Sheikh Mohammed bin Rashid Al Maktoum during her visit to Dubai in the 1970s. The UK ambassador to the UAE and Sheikh Ahmed bin Saeed Al Maktoum (centre) can be seen in the background.

OPPOSITE PAGE, BOTTOM: His Highness Sheikh Mohammed receives Margaret Thatcher during her visit to Dubai.

# Chapter 3

# Realizing a dream: 1995–2006

Following his appointment as the Crown Prince of Dubai on the January 3, 1995, His Highness Sheikh Mohammed bin Rashid Al Maktoum revealed his true character: a unique combination of modesty, confidence, futuristic vision, sternness and determination.

Introducing himself, His Highness said:

> I do not know if I am a good leader, but I am surely a leader. And I have a vision through which I can see the outlines of the future 20 or 30 years from now. I learned that from my father, the late Sheikh Rashid bin Saeed Al Maktoum, whom I consider the true father of Dubai. I strive to follow his example. He would rise early and go alone to watch what was happening on each of his projects. I do the same. I watch. I read faces. I make decisions and I move fast . . . at full throttle.

This humble self introduction only reveals limited aspects of Sheikh Mohammed's character and his unique vision that radically transformed the whole concept of development, not only in the UAE and the region, but throughout the world as well. Dubai's unique development experiment became a successful global role model many countries and cities are trying to adopt.

This development experiment took off early in 1995, when Sheikh Mohammed unveiled his vision for Dubai in the twenty-first century within the framework of the ambitious 'Dubai Vision 2010' strategy. This strategy succeeded in launching scores of gigantic infrastructure and services projects that diversified the emirate's resources away from the oil income. It also consolidated the emirate's status as an increasingly important international hub for tourism, trade, finance, business and services.

Some analysts say that when considering the gigantic projects His Highness launched, individually they seem over ambitious, but when we look at the full picture we realize that all the different initiatives complement each other, to give the emirate's and the UAE's economies a huge boost, depth and an influential role in the world.

The success of this vision materialized in the unprecedented growth the emirate witnessed in all fields and the decline in the contribution of oil and gas to less than three percent of Dubai's GDP, leading to the transformation of the new economy's sectors into the main growth engines.

This resounding success attracted widespread international interest and set an example for many countries, in and outside the region, to follow. His Highness became the symbol of enlightened leadership, endowed with vision, innovation, initiative and a pioneering spirit. In this respect His Highness says: "A man has two choices, either to be a follower or a pioneer. We are always eager to be pioneers."

**Diversifying the resources of the local economy**
Tourism was one of the main strategic components of the development vision of His Highness Sheikh Mohammed bin Rashid Al Maktoum. Realizing the importance and rapid growth of tourism at an early age, Sheikh Mohammed was confident that there was no reason at all preventing the development of this industry in Dubai. He launched the 'Destination Dubai' initiative, aiming at transforming the emirate into one of the world's favourite tourist destinations. The initiative strived to use Dubai's natural tourism resources, build up an international standard hotel industry, and organize a series of tourism, arts, sports and entertainment events, in order to promote local tourism products and the emirate's ability to attract millions of tourists from all over the world.

Launched late in 1995, the Dubai Shopping Festival proved to be one of the most successful initiatives in this respect. Thanks to its theme combining shopping with tourism, the Festival attracted huge crowds of visitors from all over the region and the world, and developed over the years to incorporate hundreds of promotional, entertainment and artistic events that meet the aspirations of all the members of visiting families.

In tandem, numerous world class championships and events were launched in Dubai, such as the Dubai World

58

Cup, the world's richest horse race attracting the world's most famous horses, the Desert Classic Golf Championship, the Dubai International Tennis Championship and many others.

The summer of 1998 witnessed the launch of the 'Dubai Summer Surprises' initiative, which proved hugely successful in energizing Dubai and the UAE's economies during the summer holiday season, when large numbers of the country's citizens and resident expatriates head overseas for quite lengthy holidays, leading to a pronounced summer lull. The event focused on entertaining children by organizing music and entertainment programs at air-conditioned shopping malls. The Summer Surprises attracted huge numbers of visitors from all over the UAE, the region and the world, and succeeded in boosting the economic activity, allowing the emirate's economy to remain buoyant throughout the year.

In order to cope with the economy's quick paced development and the consistent rise in the number of air travellers through the Dubai International Airport, the Government of Dubai embarked on a long term plan to upgrade and expand the airport. The first stage of the Sheikh Rashid Concourse was inaugurated in 1998, with the number of passengers using the airport rising to 10 million. This figure tripled by 2007 and is projected to reach 50 million by 2010.

Thus, His Highness Sheikh Mohammed bin Rashid Al Maktoum consistently proved that he was right all along, and proved his critics wrong, backed with irrefutable evidence, in the form of completed projects that seemed impossible to realize at the outset. Commenting on this success, His Highness said: "The word 'impossible' is not in the dictionaries of leaders. No matter how big the challenges, strong faith, determination and resolve will overcome them."

The hotel industry witnessed a quick paced development in its turn, and the emirate now hosts a record number and a vast variety of hotels. The government-owned Jumeirah Hotels and Resorts Group, stands witness to the emirate's success in the tourism industry. The Group opened a number of top luxurious hotels and resorts, the first of which was the superbly designed Jumeirah Beach hotel, which was inaugurated in 1997. This was soon followed by Burj Al Arab, a super luxurious hotel built in the shape of lateen sails on an artificial island. Soon thereafter, the elegantly designed Emirates twin towers were inaugurated in 2000, and became the tallest buildings in the Middle East and Africa at the time. The taller of the two towers is connected to the other by a two-storey high-end retail complex known as The Boulevard and hosts the Jumeirah Emirates Towers hotel, while the second tower is dedicated to business and corporate offices.

ABOVE: Burj Al Arab or 'The Tower of Arabs', an all-suite hotel, is located offshore on an artificial island, which was one of Sheikh Mohammed's boldest projects. Constructed in the shape of a billowing sail, it is symbolic of the Arabian heritage and culture. To the right of the picture is the Jumeirah Beach Hotel, one of Dubai's many luxury five-star hotels.

LEFT: Sheikh Mohammed on a visit to the Dubai World Trade Centre.

61

In line with the fast lane expansion policy adopted by all the groups owned by the Government of Dubai, the Jumeirah Hotel group is planning to raise the number of its resorts and hotels worldwide to 57 by 2011. The Group is presently developing several exclusive hotels in Dubai, Doha, Aqaba, Phuket, Shanghai, Bermuda and London.

**Knowledge age and the new economy**
The new knowledge economy is one of the most interesting issues in the plans of Sheikh Mohammed bin Rashid Al Maktoum, because he firmly believes that this new economy has an extremely important role to play in promoting competitiveness, at a time when trade and geographic barriers are falling. Explaining his vision in this domain His Highness says:

> At an early stage of its quick paced economic development, Dubai was keen on preparing plans that will allow it to keep pace with the developments of the new knowledge economy. So, we have decided to act on several fronts simultaneously, particularly on that of IT, the development of education and reshuffling its curricula and tools, in addition to building the appropriate infrastructure that will allow us to embrace the new knowledge economy.

His Highness affirmed that he had ambitious plans in this domain, the first of which became a reality with the Dubai e-government, aimed at upgrading the performance and services of government departments to match or even surpass the private sector's standards in this respect. In May 1999, His Highness said: "The entire Dubai government apparatus will switch to electronic government within 18 months, in order to expedite its procedures and make them smoother'. And, as a matter of fact, the Dubai e-government was up and running within the set deadline, granting Dubai a pioneering position in the region.

In October 1999, His Highness unveiled the new similarly ambitious initiative to establish the Dubai Internet City in order to boost Dubai's economy, setting a one year deadline for implementation. It was inaugurated on time indeed, offering world class electronics infrastructure, and making it the ideal choice of the world's leading IT multinationals. The city provides vital support services for all sorts of businesses, thus contributing to Dubai's already substantial competitive edge and promoting its attractiveness as a regional and international hub for multinationals.

This was followed by the launch of the Dubai Media City, an ideal media environment for media companies, including radio, television, broadcasting, production, publishing, advertising, public relations and journalism

ABOVE: Sheikh Mohammed enjoys time out at a public event.

OPPOSITE PAGE, TOP: His Highness Sheikh Mohammed touring the Dubai Mall. Also seen in the picture is His Highness Sheikh Maktoum bin Mohammed bin Rashid Al Maktoum, Deputy Ruler of Dubai.

OPPOSITE PAGE, BOTTOM: Sheikh Mohammed with Sheikh Abdullah bin Zayed Al Nahyan, the then United Arab Emirates Minister of Information and Culture, at the launch of Dubai Media City in January 2001.

over an area of 500 landscaped acres of green expanses and water fountains.

The Dubai Internet and Media cities (governed by free zone authorities), prospered over the last few years and became a vital centre hosting thousands of local, regional and multinational IT, media and telecommunications companies, such as Cisco, CNN, Compaq, IBM, Microsoft, Oracle Reuters and many more. These two 'cities' are contributing to the realization of the vision of His Highness Sheikh Mohammed bin Rashid Al Maktoum, calling for transforming Dubai into a knowledge community and economy.

Sheikh Mohammed likened the role and the importance of the knowledge economy initiatives in developing the local economy, to the efforts and the historic decision taken by Sheikh Rashid bin Saeed Al Maktoum, to dredge the navigation channel in Dubai Creek, to facilitate and promote the emirate's shipping and sea trade businesses with all the countries of the world. He explained that the projects he is presently launching, and which are aimed at shifting to a 'knowledge-based' economy, are like the other face of his late father's vision, but in a different time. In this context, His Highness said:

> We want Dubai to become a hub for the New Economy where IT companies and innovators cooperate with each other. To achieve this, we had to revise our concept of government. I will lead this shift, and since we have always wanted to be at the forefront of the world in making the shift, so why not take the initiative and be one of the first to do so?

### Real estate, construction and trade

Ever since the start of the new millennium, Sheikh Mohammed decided to sell property to residents on a freehold basis and within specific areas. Soon thereafter, the UAE's other constituent emirates and other GCC countries adopted similar policies.

The Dubai Marina and the Emirates plains real estate projects took the lead in implementing this policy, and were soon thereafter followed by scores of similar projects such as the Jumeirah Palm, the Emirates Hills, the Burj Dubai, the Gulf Business Bay and other projects, planned by many public and private property developers.

The move led to an unprecedented prosperity in the property market, and attracted a huge inflow of large investments to the local property market from all over the region and the world. The real estate industry then became one of the economy's major engines of growth, together with services industry, which witnessed a substantial growth over the last few years.

**ABOVE:** The Gate is a part of the DIFC, located off Sheikh Zayed Road beside Jumeirah Emirates Towers. This landmark building houses financial institutions, cafes and other retail and commercial outlets.

**LEFT:** Jumeirah Emirates Towers, at the heart of Dubai's commercial district, were the tallest towers in the Middle East and Africa, at the time of inauguration in 2000.

**FOLLOWING PAGE, TOP:** His Highness Sheikh Mohammed bin Rashid Al Maktoum and His Highness Sheikh Hamdan bin Mohammed Al Maktoum, the Crown Prince of Dubai, inspecting one of the Metro's carriages. Also seen in the picture are His Highnesses Sheikh Ahmed bin Mohammed Al Maktoum and Musbeh Al Fattan.

**FOLLOWING PAGE, BOTTOM:** The Dubai Metro project is one of the most prestigious infrastructural projects in the Middle East. The mega project was implemented in record time, in line with the world's highest standards.

Top: Emirates airline grew at a tremendous pace and is now one of the world's largest and fastest growing airlines. Seen in the picture is the 'double-decker' Airbus A380, of which Emirates airline ordered 54 aircraft.

Above: An aerial view of the new developments dotting Dubai's coastline, showing, from left to right, the Palm Jebel Ali, the Palm Jumeirah, The World, the Palm Deira and the expansion project of the Creek.

ABOVE: This photograph clearly illustrates the affection that His Highness Sheikh Mohammed and His Highness Sheikh Maktoum shared for one another.

RIGHT: Seen here from right to left, Sheikh Mohammed bin Rashid Al Maktoum, Sheikh Hamdan bin Rashid Al Maktoum, Deputy Ruler of Dubai and the Minister of Finance and Sheikh Maktoum bin Rashid Al Maktoum, enjoying a festive event.

FOLLOWING PAGE, TOP: Sheikh Zayed bin Sultan Al Nahyan arriving at the palace of Sheikh Maktoum bin Rashid Al Maktoum at Nad Al Sheba in Dubai for a banquet, attended by their Highnesses, the Rulers of the emirates. His Highness Sheikh Mohammed bin Rashid Al Maktoum, the Vice-President, Prime Minister and Ruler of Dubai, is seen to the right. In the first row right behind them are seen from right to left, Sheikh Saqr bin Sultan Al Qasimi and Sheikh Rashid bin Ahmed Al Mualla. In the second row from left to right are, Sheikh Hamad bin Mohammed Al Sharqi, Ruler of Fujairah, and Sheikh Humaid bin Rashid Al Nuaimi, Ruler of Ajman.

FOLLOWING PAGE, BOTTOM: Sheikh Mohammed in conversation with Sheikh Rashid bin Ahmed Al Mualla, while to the extreme left of the picture is His Highness Sheikh Khalifa bin Zayed Al Nahyan, the President and Supreme Commander of the Armed Forces, Ruler of Abu Dhabi, and to his left in the background is His Highness Sheikh Sultan bin Mohammed bin Sultan Al Qasimi, Crown Prince and Deputy Ruler of Sharjah. Also seen in the background, to the left of His Highness Sheikh Mohammed, is His Highness Sheikh Ammar bin Humaid bin Rashid Al Nuaimi, Crown Prince of Ajman.

In the meantime, strong investment in infrastructural projects contributed to promoting the emirate's status as a regional trade hub serving a huge geographical region extending between North and East Africa and the Indian subcontinent and the Commonwealth of Independent States. Foreign trade figures, on the other hand, kept growing by two-figure rates over the past ten years.

**The financial hub of the Middle East**
The year 2002 witnessed the launch of a new initiative that contributed to consolidating the emirate's international financial and business status. His Highness Sheikh Mohammed announced a project to establish the Dubai International Financial Centre, in order to bridge the time slot between the West and East's international financial centres and consolidate Dubai's status as an international financial hub that provides a world class business environment, based on stringent international standards and opening its doors to foreign investors searching for an opportunity to access regional and world capital markets.

During its first few years of operation, the Centre attracted the world's major banks and financial institutions, and was widely considered as a trustworthy international financial centre, allowing the customers of its corporate members to trade across a geographical area extending across the Indian subcontinent and East and North African countries and the West.

The opening of the Centre came at an ideal time that preceded an accelerated economic development period throughout the entire region, thus reflecting the vision of Sheikh Mohammed bin Rashid Al Maktoum and calling for a comprehensive development combining daring, ambitious and quick response.

**The beginning of a new era**
Amidst all these amazing achievements that sowed a climate of optimism, the UAE was shocked by the sudden death of Sheikh Maktoum on January 4, 2006, while on a private visit to Australia.

The Supreme Council of the Rulers of the Emirates convened the day following the tragic event to discuss appointing a successor for His Highness Sheikh Maktoum bin Rashid Al Maktoum, in his capacities as the Vice-President and Prime Minister of the UAE. Unanimously on January 6, 2009, the appointment of His Highness Sheikh Mohammed bin Rashid Al Maktoum, as the Vice-President and Prime Minister of the UAE was approved. He also succeeded his late brother as the Ruler of Dubai and retained his ministerial portfolio as the Defence Minister of the UAE.

ABOVE: Noor Ali Rashid's last photo of Sheikh Maktoum, taken during a meeting of the Supreme Council at Al Bateen Palace a month before he passed away; he is seen standing to the right of His Highness Sheikh Khalifa bin Zayed Al Nahyan, while Sheikh Mohammed is seen second to the right of the picture. Also seen in the photo, from left to right, are: Sheikh Saud bin Rashid Al Mualla, Member of the Supreme Council, Ruler of Umm al-Quwain; Sheikh Hamad bin Saif Al Sharqi, Deputy Ruler of Fujairah; Sheikh Ammar bin Humaid bin Rashid Al Nuaimi, Crown Prince of Ajman; Sheikh Hamdan bin Rashid Al Maktoum, Deputy Ruler of Dubai, Finance Minister; Sheikh Saud bin Saqr Al Qasimi, Member of the Supreme Council, Ruler of Ra's al-Khaimah; Sheikh Humaid bin Rashid Al Nuaimi, Ruler of Ajman; Sheikh Sultan bin Mohammed Al Qasimi, Member of the Supreme Council, Ruler of Sharjah; Sheikh Hamad bin Mohammed Al Sharqi, Member of the Supreme Council, Ruler of Fujairah; Sheikh Rashid bin Ahmed Al Mualla; Sheikh Abdullah bin Rashid Al Mualla, Member of the Supreme Council, Ruler of Umm al-Qaiwain; Sheikh Mohammed bin Zayed Al Nahyan, Crown Prince of Abu Dhabi, Deputy Supreme Commander of the Armed Forces and Sheikh Sultan bin Mohammed bin Sultan Al Qasimi, Crown Prince and Deputy Ruler of Sharjah.

RIGHT: Sheikh Mohammed with the Crown Prince of Ajman, Sheikh Ammar bin Humaid Al Nuaimi, on the day of Sheikh Ammar's wedding.

# Chapter 4

# A new portfolio: 2006 to date

When Sheikh Mohammed assumed his functions as the Vice-President and Prime Minister of the UAE and Ruler of Dubai on January 6, 2006, the United Arab Emirates was ushered into a new era of development and progress.

The formation of the new government, the seventh in the country's history since its establishment in 1971, topped the priorities of Sheikh Mohammed's agenda. He was keen on forming a highly efficient government, allowing a larger spectrum of citizens to contribute to the country's public life and upgrade the services of many vital sectors, such as education, healthcare, social affairs and the economy, within the framework of a responsibility and accountability system.

At the new cabinet's first meeting, presided by His Highness Sheikh Mohammed, he clearly stressed that the ministers should adopt a positive and interactive stance, by not merely reporting to him the obstacles obstructing the proper functioning of their ministries, but by suggesting a number of solutions to overcome them as well.

From the beginning, Sheikh Mohammed emphasized the need for a radical change in the performance of all federal ministries, institutions and organizations. The change happened and was highly successful. He further established a new system of dealing with public affairs, by taking the entire cabinet to unusual venues to hold intensive meetings that took one or two days. The ministers were not allowed to bring their mobile phones with them, so that they remain focused and concentrate on the business at hand.

## The strategy of the federal government

As announced by Sheikh Mohammed on April 17, 2007, the strategy of the new federal government focused on six major sectors, mainly community development, economic development, justice and safety development, government development, infrastructural development and remote areas development. The strategy revolved around the following principles: promoting better cooperation and coordination

between the federal and local authorities, activating governance in ministries, developing the mechanisms of policy and decision making, upgrading the efficacy and efficiency of government bodies, upgrading the standards of services with a focus on satisfying customers, development of the civil service laws, developing human resources by emphasizing qualification and merit and empowering the second generation leaderships. These principles also involved granting ministries more independence in managing their affairs within the framework of commitment to the general policies and integral performance and revising and updating the prevailing laws.

At the economic level, the strategy particularly focused on promoting competitiveness of the local economy,

---

PREVIOUS SPREAD: Sheikh Khalifa and Sheikh Mohammed bin Rashid Al Maktoum seen with the seventh UAE Cabinet formed by Sheikh Mohammed and announced on February 9, 2006.

FRONT ROW FROM LEFT TO RIGHT: Mariam Mohammed Khalfan Al Roumi, Minister of Social Affairs; Sheikh Hamdan bin Mubarak Al Nahyan, Minister of Public Works; Sheikh Abdullah bin Zayed Al Nahyan, Foreign Minister; Sheikh Hamdan bin Zayed Al Nahyan, Deputy Prime Minister; Sheikh Mohammed bin Rashid Al Maktoum, Vice-President and Prime Minister of the UAE and Ruler of Dubai; Sheikh Khalifa bin Zayed Al Nahyan, President of the UAE and Ruler of Abu Dhabi; Sheikh Sultan bin Zayed Al Nahyan, Deputy Prime Minister; Sheikh Hamdan bin Rashid Al Maktoum, Minister of Finance and Industry; Lieutenant Sheikh Saif bin Zayed Al Nahyan, Minister of Interior; Sheikh Mansour bin Zayed Al Nahyan, Minister of Presidential Affairs; Sheikh Nahayan bin Mabarak Al Nahayan, Minister of Higher Education and Scientific Research; and Sheikha Lubna Al Qasimi, Minister of Economy.

BACK ROW FROM LEFT TO RIGHT: Dr Mohammed Saeed Al Kindi, Minister of Environment and Water; Dr Anwar Mohammed Gargash, Minister of State for Federal National Council Affairs; Humaid Mohammed Obaid Al Qutami, Minister of Health; Mohammed Abdullah Al Gergawi, Minister of State for Cabinet Affairs; Dr Ali bin Abdullah Al Ka'abi, Minister of Labour; Dr Mohammed Khalfan bin Kharbash, Minister of State for Financial and Industrial Affairs; Mohammed bin Nakhira Al Dhahiri, Minister of Justice; Mohammed bin Dha'en Al Hamili, Minister of Energy; Sultan bin Saeed Al Mansour, Minister of Government Sector Development; Mohammed Hussain Al Sha'ali, Minister of State for Foreign Affairs; Dr Hanif Hassan, Minister of Education; and Abdul Rahman Mohammed Al Owais, Minister of Culture, Youth and Community Development.

OPPOSITE PAGE: UAE President Sheikh Khalifa and Sheikh Mohammed meet in December 2005, shortly before Sheikh Mohammed became Vice-President and Prime Minister of the United Arab Emirates and Ruler of Dubai following the sudden death of his brother, Sheikh Maktoum.

---

updating economic laws and legislations and empowering their implementation, promoting federal government's governance role, energizing the process of formulating and implementing financial and trade policies and developing corporate governance.

Outlining the government's priorities, His Highness said:

> We are determined to achieve a great renaissance in all domains, in a way that will lead to upgrading the education system to the highest standards, infrastructure and service sectors to the highest international standards and government performance excellence to the best international practices. And while political empowering shall continue by granting more powers to the national federal council, in order to promote its role in national affairs and reaffirm the commitment to a consultative government system, economic empowering will also continue through upgrading legislation, promoting a better business environment, upgrading quality and competitiveness standards and focusing on developing the basic production and services sectors.

"Social empowering will also go on forward through the development of our human resources by providing better education and training, developing the process of job emiratization, expanding the reach of housing programs and promoting women's contribution to the development process and building the nation. We are driven by a strong will to promote better integration between the federal and local authorities, upgrading the efficiency of government bodies through an active implementation of the government's strategy, developing civil service legislations and the structures of the Ministries and other government agencies", His Highness added.

In February 2008, a major cabinet reshuffle was announced; seven new ministers assumed their functions, with the number of women ministers doubling from two to four. This was the first major cabinet reshuffle since His Highness Sheikh Mohammed bin Rashid Al Maktoum became the UAE's Prime Minister two years before, in January 2006. The reshuffle aimed at promoting the government's flexibility and its ability to quickly respond to the requirements of development.

In this respect, His Highness said: "God wanted me to bear witness to the events of December 2, 1971, and before that to the strenuous efforts exerted to establish the Union, ever since the famous February 1968 meeting at (Arqoob Al Sudeirah), where the two founding fathers of the nation, agreed to establish a federation between their two emirates, Abu Dhabi and Dubai. Every time I witness another second of December, I recall the events of our blessed federation, with all its episodes, personalities and symbols, and feel more confident and more thankful to God the All Mighty and the All Merciful, for the blessings, success, progress and development he accorded us. Every year that elapses following December 2, the memory reel becomes longer and its pictures become clearer and more coherent, and I can then realize how gigantic, monumental and historical the achievement of that day was . . .

Despite their importance, uniqueness, excellence and their matching of the highest international standards, I am not talking here about the construction achievements only, but I am also talking about our strategic achievements that changed the geopolitical map of the region, by establishing a new state willingly and freely uniting seven entities. Those achievements also changed the social geography of the region, by establishing a new community and a new identity. They further changed the region's intellectual geography through establishing a promising federal model in the Arab region, whose peoples are eager for federation, although hurt by the failure of previous models. Year after year, those huge historical achievements look brighter, gain more status and become an example worth following, for the simple reason of the prosperity

they brought to our nation and its evident ambition for more achievements."

**Establishing the regional and international status of the United Arab Emirates**

Led by Sheikh Mohammed, the government strived to strengthen the policies adopted by the United Arab Emirates since its inception, consisting of playing a positive and efficient role within its Gulf and Arab environment, and on the international stage as well.

The country's foreign policy calls for supporting and promoting common Gulf action and strengthening relations with the GCC countries in all fields. It also calls for continued support of Arab and Islamic causes, strengthening relations with developed countries, helping underdeveloped nations and supporting international organizations. This policy helped promote the UAE's regional and international status and role. This explains the frequent visits paid by some of the world's most prominent leaders to the country.

His Highness Sheikh Mohammed bin Rashid Al Maktoum also made several official visits to many countries over the last few years, including UK, Germany, China, India, South Korea, Vietnam among others.

ABOVE: His Highness Sheikh Khalifa bin Zayed, the President of the UAE and the Supreme Commander of the Armed Forces, presiding over a meeting of the Supreme Council of their Highnesses the Rulers of the constituent emirates. Seen to his right, is His Highness Sheikh Mohammed bin Rashid Al Maktoum, Vice-President and Prime Minister of the UAE and Ruler of Dubai, while His Highness Dr Sheikh Sultan bin Mohammed Al Qasimi, Member of the Supreme Council and Ruler of Sharjah is seen sitting to his left.

OPPOSITE PAGE, TOP: His Highnesses Sheikh Khalifa and Sheikh Mohammed, and Members of the Supreme Council, at one of their regular and frequent consultative meetings.

OPPOSITE PAGE, BOTTOM: His Highness Sheikh Mohammed bin Rashid Al Maktoum, presiding over a meeting of the Council of Ministers.

The United Arab Emirates plays a vital role in strengthening regional cooperation.

Top: Sheikh Mohammed with King Abdullah bin Abdulaziz Al Saud of Saudi Arabia, who succeeded to the throne in 2005. King Abdullah, who is also the Prime Minister of Saudi Arabia, is the fifth son of King Abdulaziz bin Abdulrahman Al Saud, the founder of modern Saudi Arabia, to ascend to the throne.

Above: His Highness Sheikh Mohammed bin Rashid Al Maktoum with King Hamad bin Eisa Al Khalifa of Bahrain. In the second row are Sheikh Tahnoun bin Mohammed Al Nahyan and Sheikh Suroor bin Mohammed Al Nahyan.

Top: Sheikh Mohammed with the Emir of Qatar, Sheikh Hamad bin Khalifa Al Thani.

Above: Sheikh Mohammed with Sheikh Sabah Al Ahmed Al Jaber Al Sabah, the head of Kuwait's Ruling Al Sabah family, who has been Emir since 2006.

ABOVE: Sheikh Mohammed with King Abdullah II of Jordan at Za'abeel Palace.

OPPOSITE PAGE, TOP: Sheikh Mohammed greets Sultan Qaboos during one of his visits to Dubai. The United Arab Emirates and Oman are two of the founder members of the Gulf Cooperation Council (GCC), founded in 1981.

OPPOSITE PAGE, BOTTOM LEFT: Sheikh Mohammed with the President of Algeria, Abdelaziz Bouteflika, who was elected President in 1999 and re-elected for a second term in 2004.

OPPOSITE PAGE, BOTTOM RIGHT: Sheikh Mohammed with King Mohammed VI of Morocco, who has ruled the kingdom since 1999. King Mohammed is known as a modernizer.

ABOVE LEFT: Sheikh Mohammed with Syrian President Bashar Al Assad, on a tour of the Dubai Air Show 2000.

ABOVE RIGHT: Sheikh Mohammed with Dr Ahmed Nazeef, the Prime Minister of Egypt since 2004.

TOP RIGHT: Sheikh Mohammed is seen here with former Prime Minister and current President of Palestine, Mahmoud Abbas.

OPPOSITE PAGE, TOP: Sheikh Mohammed at a meeting with the President of Tunisia, Zine El Abidene Ben Ali, who has been in office since 1987.

OPPOSITE PAGE, BOTTOM: Sheikh Mohammed with the Prime Minister of Lebanon, Rafik Hariri to his right, while to his left is Sheikh Ahmed bin Saeed Al Maktoum, Chairman and Chief Executive Emirates Airline & Group. Sitting to the right of the Rafik Hariri is Ahmed Al Tayer.

Dubai enjoys close relations with non-Arab and non-Islamic countries. His Highness Sheikh Mohammed regularly meets with leaders of these countries, who contribute to shaping our world and its future.

RIGHT: Sheikh Mohammed bin Rashid Al Maktoum shaking hands with the British Prime Minister, Gordon Brown outside 10 Downing Street, the official residence of the United Kingdom's Prime Minister.

BELOW: Sheikh Mohammed with Tony Blair, Prime Minister of the United Kingdom from 1997 to 2007 (the Labour Party's longest serving Prime Minister). Tony Blair is currently the Official Envoy of the Quartet on the Middle East on behalf of the United Nations, the European Union, the United States and Russia.

OPPOSITE PAGE, TOP: Sheikh Mohammed, accompanying US President George W. Bush on a visit to Dubai early in 2008, on a tour to show him some of the city's heritage areas including Sheikh Saeed House.

OPPOSITE PAGE, BOTTOM: Sheikh Mohammed hosting President Bush to an Arabic dinner, in a traditional *majlis*.

ABOVE: His Highness Sheikh Mohammed with the former German Chancellor Gerhard Schroeder.

RIGHT: Sheikh Mohammed greeting Mikhail Gorbachev, the last head of state of the USSR.

OPPOSITE PAGE, TOP: His Highness Sheikh Mohammed bin Rashid Al Maktoum in a meeting with the Turkish Prime Minister Rejeb Tayyeb Erdogan.

OPPOSITE PAGE, BOTTOM: Sheikh Mohammed inspecting a Vietnamese guard of honour with the country's progressive Prime Minister, Nguyen Tan Dung – the youngest Prime Minister to hold office in the socialist republic.

TOP LEFT: Sheikh Mohammed and Philippine President, Gloria Arroyo, discuss promoting mutual cooperation between the two countries in Dubai in 2008.

TOP RIGHT: Sheikh Mohammed discussing matters of mutual interest with President Mahmoud Ahmadinejad of Iran.

ABOVE LEFT: Sheikh Mohammed with Pervez Musharraf of Pakistan, the ex-President of Pakistan.

ABOVE RIGHT: Sheikh Mohammed with President Hamid Karzai of Afghanistan.

OPPOSITE PAGE, TOP LEFT: Sheikh Mohammed with the Indian politician Sonia Gandhi, widow of the former Prime Minister of India, Rajiv Gandhi, son of the Indian Prime Minister Indira Gandhi and the grandchild of the Indian leader Jawaharlal Nehru.

OPPOSITE PAGE, TOP RIGHT: Sheikh Mohammed with Manmohan Singh, the Prime Minister of India.

OPPOSITE PAGE, BELOW: Sheikh Mohammed with the former Prime Minister of India, Rajiv Gandhi, who was assassinated and died in 1991.

ABOVE: Sheikh Mohammed in discussion with the former US Secretary of State, General Colin Powell, who served under US President George W. Bush.

RIGHT: Sheikh Mohammed presents the Zayed International Prize for Global Leadership for the Environment to the former UN Secretary-General, Kofi Annan, in Dubai in 2006.

OPPOSITE PAGE, TOP: Sheikh Mohammed accompanying the former US President, Bill Clinton and his daughter Chelsea, at a graduation ceremony at the American University in Dubai.

OPPOSITE PAGE, BOTTOM: Sheikh Mohammed presenting the Sheikh Zayed International Prize for Global Leadership for the Environment to the former US President Jimmy Carter in April 2001.

His Highness Sheikh Mohammed enjoying a traditional luncheon with Prince Philippe and Princess Mathilde of Belgium during the royal couple's visit to Dubai in 2004.

His Highness Sheikh Mohammed bin Rashid Al Maktoum with Nelson Mandela, the former President of South Africa.

# Chapter 5

# New achievements

His Highness Sheikh Mohammed bin Rashid Al Maktoum, Vice-President and Prime Minister of the UAE and Ruler of Dubai, bolstered the achievements and initiatives he launched in the previous years since he assumed his functions, by realizing a sustainable development and promoting Dubai and the UAE's status as an increasingly important international hub. Outlining his development vision in this respect, His Highness said:

> Our plans are not driven by ambition but rather by necessity. We must understand that while dwindling crude oil export revenues only represent three per cent of our income, 30 per cent of that income comes from tourism. Moreover, an increasing share of our income is now being derived from manufacturing and other industries, such as hospitality, technology, transport and communications.

"Since some people refer to the emirate as Dubai Corporation or Dubai Inc., it implies that trade is the prevailing industry and nothing else. Yes, that is definitely true, because over several centuries, Dubai represented an important trading port and hub. But Dubai's soul and mood were and are still based on building bridges with the outside world, and establishing relations and connections with different cultures and civilizations. In my childhood, I learned the importance of establishing a strong economy, in which the government offers incentives and provides a regulatory environment based on ethics, while the private sector is left with the task of accelerating economic development, using its substantial energies and innovative capacity." His Highness added.

"I have learned my 'own capitalism' in Dubai's traditional souks and streets, and perhaps the main lesson I learned was to always ask: how can we become tools and factors of change? This is why I prefer to describe Dubai as the 'incentive corporation' or the 'incentivizing Dubai Inc.'. We are living in a difficult region and in a state surrounded by complex problems such as the Iraq-Iran war, the invasion of Kuwait and the ongoing war in Iraq. Despite all this, Dubai has always learned how to reintroduce itself in an innovative way."

This creative vision promoted Sheikh Mohammed's status as an international symbol of progress, modernity and creative achievements and led *Time* magazine to nominate him among the world's personalities most able to change the world through their power, talents and idealistic ethics.

The development strategy adopted by His Highness has been a tremendous success, making Dubai a driving engine for change and progress throughout the region and a global example worth following.

**A global aviation hub**

In his capacity as the Ruler of Dubai, one of the first decisions Sheikh Mohammed adopted, was to establish the Dubai Aviation Industries Corporation, aiming at investing up to Dhs 55 billion in the aviation industry, including the manufacturing and assembly of aircraft components and spare parts. Furthermore, he launched a series of major infrastructural projects, including roads, power and water stations and sanitation projects. These projects were accompanied by consistent efforts to upgrade regulations and legislations and create an ideal environment conducive to the development of businesses.

In a speech he delivered at the Arabian Travel Market in Dubai, he unveiled his master plan to turn Dubai into a global civil aviation hub, only two months following his assuming his functions as the Ruler of Dubai. The plan unveiled the Al Maktoum International Airport project, aimed at building the world's largest airport.

Describing the project and its relation with the development of Dubai, His Highness Sheikh Ahmed bin Saeed Al Maktoum Chairman of the Dubai Civil Aviation Department, Chairman and Chief Executive of Emirates Airline & Group said: "the second wave of development projects will include the establishment of a true global trade, aviation and logistics hub."

The project's stunning statistics reveal the gigantic dimensions of the projects entertained by His Highness

**ABOVE: His Highness Sheikh Mohammed bin Rashid Al Maktoum visits the headquarters of
Emirates Group in Dubai.**

**FOLLOWING PAGE: Sheikh Mohammed presiding over a meeting of the Dubai 2020 committee, in
charge of the file concerning Dubai's bid to host the 2020 Olympic Games. Also seen in the
picture are their Highnesses, Sheikh Hamdan bin Mohammed Al Maktoum, the Crown Prince
of Dubai and the Chairman of Dubai's Executive Council; Sheikh Ahmed bin Mohammed Al
Maktoum, Chairman of the Mohammed bin Rashid Al Maktoum Foundation; and a number of
Dubai government departmental heads.**

Sheikh Mohammed and his vision of the future. The new airport will be dotted with six runways and will handle 120 million passengers and 12 million tonnes of air cargo a year. These figures are much higher than those dealt by either London's Heathrow or Chicago's O'Hare airports.

Once the huge infrastructure of this giant airport are completed and assisted by the nearby Dubai Logistics City and Jebel Ali port and Free Zone, it will accommodate Dubai's civil aviation, trade, tourism and logistics requirements well into 2050. Commenting on the project, Sheikh Mohammed said: "We must make history and steadily race against future challenges, instead of waiting for the future to come to us."

Meanwhile, Emirates airline was making giant strides and consistently increasing its profits. This bold national carrier did not stop at ordering 45 Airbus A 380 double-decker super jumbo jets for Dhs 70 billion, at the Dubai Air Show 2005 in the largest ever order of its kind in the history of civil aviation, but added eight more similar aircraft to its original order at the Paris Air Show the same year. Thus, the total number of confirmed aircraft orders the carrier had on its books early in 2008 reached 245 aircraft.

In other fields and based on the Dubai vision 2010 strategic plan, the emirate kept attracting investments to its advanced knowledge and hi-tech complexes, such as the Dubai Internet and Media cities, Dubai Knowledge Village, Dubai International Airport Free Zone, Dubai Healthcare City, Dubai International Financial Centre, Dubai Maritime City, Dubai Technology Complex among others. As a result, Dubai enjoyed an unprecedented growth, led by a sound futuristic vision and a unique planning for success.

When Sheikh Mohammed bin Rashid Al Maktoum formulated his Dubai vision 2010 master plan setting the outlines for the development of the emirate's economy, only a handful of people were able to visualize the shape of the future and the ways to implement these ambitious projects. The plans nevertheless succeeded in building a modern developed society and laid strong foundations for pioneering new peaks of excellence in the future.

While elaborating on his ambitious plans during his announcement of the Dubailand mega project, His Highness Sheikh Mohammed bin Rashid Al Maktoum said:

> Those pondering these projects as independent ones, will never understand their true potential. These projects constitute a continuous chain of elements that form an integral part of a clear and comprehensive strategic vision. They will further never understand that Dubai has what it takes to become a highly attractive global tourism destination, capable of attracting millions of tourists.

Thanks to the pioneering ideas of Sheikh Mohammed and the well-orchestrated development projects he launched; aviation, tourism, education, IT, healthcare and real estate topped the emirate's development agenda, and together gave its economy a formidable momentum and clout.

### Dubai's strategic plan 2015

In February 2007, Sheikh Mohammed announced the 'Dubai Vision 2015' strategic plan. Elaborating on the plan, His Highness said:

> When I announced my vision for Dubai in the year 2000, I spoke of economic aims for the year 2010. The reality is not only that these aims have been realized but that they have been realized in half the time[1]. Dubai Strategic Plan will open a new page in our history after the successful execution of the first one. It will position Dubai as a leading Arab and global city as the government provides the growth engine for the public and investors alike.

"Those achievements would have not been possible, if it were not for our insistence on challenging ourselves, consolidating our resources and channelling them in the right direction, in order to better serve our initiatives, projects and programs in all integral development fields. Those superior achievements are mainly due to government initiatives. The government always realized the importance of investing in the emirate and consistently developing its business environment. This is evident in the government's efforts to modernize and upgrade the efficiency of its services, its institutional structure and the emirate's legislations, regulations and infrastructure. Those efforts involved launching strategic projects such as tourism and construction projects, the Dubai Internet and Media cities, the Dubai International Financial Centre, the specialized free zones and many more," His Highness added.

"Those initiatives formed the driving force of development and the main factor in attracting investments. They encouraged the private sector, promoted its confidence and put huge opportunities at its disposal, driving it to catch up with the government efforts and projects, until it became a true development partner. Over the last few years, we have accomplished the extremely important achievement of restructuring the economy. The

---

[1]The Dubai 2000 plan envisaged raising the emirate's GDP to Dhs 110 billion by 2010, but as a matter of fact that figure was surpassed in 2005, when the GDP shot to Dhs 135 billion, while the Dubai 2015 plan aimed at raising the GDP to Dhs 296 billion. Dubai's per capita income matched this large increase in the emirate's GDP with similar rates.

contribution of the non-oil sectors to the local economy rose to 97 per cent against 90 per cent in 2000 and around 46 per cent in 1975," His Highness explained.

"Our success in diversifying our sources of income made up for our limited oil reserves and revenues, protecting our economic development from the direct impact of oil revenues. This is an historical achievement that may be useful to other oil producing countries seeking to restructure their economies in order to diversify their income sources. We were in a race against time and won the race. But as I have always said, the race has just begun and our achievements impose on us new responsibilities and serious tasks that the strategic plan for 2015 is trying to shoulder," His Highness added.

The new plan is divided into five spheres of activity: economic development, social development, infrastructure, land and environment, safety, security and justice and public sector excellence. The plan deals with those spheres of action in a strategic manner that emphasizes the development of the emirate's most dynamic economic sectors and focuses on major concerns that faced Dubai's residents over the last few years, such as traffic congestion, rent hikes and inflation.

Since such an unprecedented growth needs strict controls and an ingenious leadership, which Dubai and the UAE already enjoys, the pioneering policies of His Highness Sheikh Mohammed became the focus of an increasing local, regional and international interest. The idea of a developed modern country in the Middle East was warmly welcomed by governments, multinational majors and businessmen overseas, with a large number of them deciding to establish a presence in the UAE.

It encompasses some of the aspects of the bold targets set by Sheikh Mohammed's vision – based on setting ambitious goals – providing all the resources needed to accomplish them, in order to thereafter embark on achieving more ambitious goals. In this respect, His Highness said:

_____

OPPOSITE PAGE, TOP: **Sheikh Mohammed reviewing the model of a new project. Seen to his right is Sheikh Nahayan bin Mabarak Al Nahayan, Minister of Higher Education and Scientific Research.**

OPPOSITE PAGE, BOTTOM: **His Highness reviewing the plans of one of the projects, implemented by Dubai Municipality.**

**OPPOSITE PAGE, TOP:** Sheikh Mohammed conferring with Sheikh Ahmed, Chairman of the Dubai Civil Aviation Department, Chairman and Chief Executive of Emirates Airline & Group .

**OPPOSITE PAGE, BOTTOM:** Sheikh Mohammed watching an emission of the 'Dubai Sat' Communications satellite.

**THIS PAGE, TOP:** Sheikh Mohammed pushing the activation button of the Dubai Metro. Seen to the left behind him, is His Highness Sheikh Hamdan bin Mohammed bin Rashid Al Maktoum.

**THIS PAGE, CENTRE:** Sheikh Mohammed with Mohammed Al Shibani, Director General of the Court of His Highness the Ruler of Dubai.

**THIS PAGE, BOTTOM:** Sheikh Mohammed touring the Al Arabi Shopping Centre. Also seen are His Highnesses Sheikh Hamdan and Sheikh Maktoum; and Lieutenant General Musabah Al Fattan.

We never were and shall never be like those who sleep over their successes, are satisfied by their achievements or believe that progress shall be self driven. Life never stops and does not pay attention to those who stand idle, because every new day brings with it new tasks, problems and challenges, science, knowledge, inventions and new means. He, who omits even for one second catching up with new developments and does not persevere in his striving to reach the front row, will be left in the back rows. And he, who leaves to chance doing things for him, will lament his bad luck one of these days. Moreover, he who leaves to time to manage his affairs will discover that time is not neutral. Time only befriends those who work, seek and take initiatives and is the enemy of those who sleep, rely on others, neglect their duties or are simply lazy.

Early in 2008, Sheikh Mohammed appointed his sons, Sheikh Hamdan and Sheikh Maktoum, while his own brother His Highness Sheikh Hamdan bin Rashid Al Maktoum retained his position as Deputy Ruler of Dubai.

His Highness Sheikh Hamdan attended the Rashid private school in Dubai, before graduating from the Sandhurst Royal Military College, the London Economic School and the Dubai Government College. He represents a new breed of rulers, because of his young age and exemplary academic and sports achievements, in addition to his experience in managing government and private sector affairs. These elements together endow Sheikh Hamdan bin Mohammed Al Maktoum with excellent credits for assuming his leadership functions.

Ever since the late 1950s, Dubai's success story adopted a strategy based upon an efficient partnership between the public and private sectors. This allowed the government to grant the priority to the development of infrastructure and providing a legislative and legal environment conducive to the development and prosperity of businesses.

This strategy proved hugely successful and became the main driving engine of the emirate's development into a major regional trade hub during the tenure of Sheikh Rashid bin Saeed Al Maktoum. This strategy took new dimensions during the reign of His Highness Sheikh Mohammed bin Rashid Al Maktoum, who was always keen on meeting with businessmen, because he believed in the importance if incentivizing the private sector in order to turn it into a full partner in the development process.

This page, top: Sheikh Mohammed in a friendly chat with Sultan Al Owais, the son of a pearl trader and the first Chairman of the National Bank of Dubai.

This page, centre: Sheikh Mohammed in a friendly meeting with Abdul Aziz Abdullah Al Ghurair (left), the speaker of the National federal Council, the CEO of the UAE-based Mashreqbank which was started by his father, and Abdulla Ahmed Al Ghurair (right).

This page, bottom: Sheikh Mohammed standing with Abdullah Saleh, the then Chairman of the National Bank of Dubai.

Opposite page, top left: Sheikh Mohammed in a meeting with Khalaf Al Habtoor, Chairman, Al Habtoor Group, Dubai.

Opposite page, top right: Sheikh Mohammed in discussion with Saeed Al Naboodah, the former President of the Dubai Chamber of Commerce and Industry.

Opposite page, centre left: Sheikh Mohammed with Abdulla Hamad Al Futtaim, Chairman of the Al Futtaim Group, looking at the: *Dubai – A Pictorial Tour* book.

Opposite page, centre right: Sheikh Mohammed meeting with Majid Al Futtaim, brother of Abdulla Hamad Al Futtaim and President of the Majid Al Futtaim Group.

Opposite page, bottom left: Sheikh Mohammed in a meeting with Sheikha Lubna Al Qasimi, the UAE Minister for Economy (the first woman to hold a ministerial post in the UAE) and Mohammed Al Naboodah.

Opposite page, bottom right: Sheikh Mohammed with the Director General of Dubai Police Lieutenant General Dahi Khalfan Tamim (centre) and Helal Saeed Al Marri (left), Director General, the Dubai World Trade centre.

# Chapter 6

# A father to his family and people

His Highness Sheikh Mohammed bin Rashid Al Maktoum represents a unique breed of leaders, for despite his huge responsibilities as the Vice-President and Prime Minister of the UAE and Ruler of Dubai, he always dedicates some of his time each day to follow up the affairs of his compatriots, share their celebrations and grief and strive to solve their problems, which makes him a father to his family and people.

Although Sheikh Mohammed's daily schedule is often filled with official meetings and receptions, this never prevents him from receiving his countrymen at his *majlis*, or even paying a home visit to some citizens, either to share their celebration of a wedding or their grief for the loss of a dear one. Sheikh Mohammed also regularly tours all the emirates and directly meets with people, listens to their grievances and problems and issues instructions to attend to them.

Sheikh Mohammed's upbringing was characterized by strong family ties, and he was intent on educating his children in a similar environment. Thus we see Sheikh Mohammed's children closely accompanying him at official events and whenever he meets government officials and citizen at his *majlis*.

He is also keen on dedicating some of his time to his family to share in their hobbies, led by horsemanship and poetry. Sheikh Mohammed and his children are all accomplished and renowned poets and also horse racing champions, winning many gold medals at regional and international endurance races. Recalling his family upbringing, he says:

> My parents loved me and I loved them. Since God The All Mighty and The All Merciful blessed me with sons and daughters, I would like them to love me just like I love them. I am however different from other people in that I let the moment control my feelings, so that I become a leader when I lead, a poet when I compose poems and an ordinary citizen when I meet with my compatriots.

Sheikh Mohammed was eager to teach his children the need to shoulder the huge responsibilities imposed on them by their commitment to their country and people, the same responsibilities he shouldered since his childhood. He was also keen on educating his children at the best colleges. His eldest son, Sheikh Rashid, graduated from Sandhurst Military Academy, as well as his second son, Sheikh Hamdan, who was appointed Crown Price of Dubai and Chairman of the Dubai Executive Council, while his third son, Sheikh Maktoum, a graduate of the American University in Dubai, was appointed the Deputy Ruler of Dubai.

ABOVE: Sheikh Mohammed and his son, Sheikh Hamdan, peruse the first copy of Noor Ali Rashid's book *Sheikh Maktoum – Life and Times.*

The two great Arabian dynasties, the Al Nahyans and the Al Maktoums led by His Highness Sheikh Khalifa bin Zayed Al Nahyan, the President, Supreme Commander of the Armed Forces, Ruler of Abu Dhabi, and His Highness Sheikh Mohammed bin Rashid Al Maktoum, the Vice- President, Prime Minister and Ruler of Dubai entertained a very close relationship nurtured by the two founding fathers of the nation, Sheikh Zayed bin Sultan Al Nahyan and Sheikh Rashid bin Saeed Al Maktoum. Their sons further bolstered those relations, thus securing the continued prosperity of the United Arab Emirates. These two rare photographs highlight how deep and strong those relations were.

Above: Sheikh Zayed bin Sultan Al Nahyan with three of the Al Maktoum brothers (from right to left) – Sheikh Mohammed bin Rashid Al Maktoum, Sheikh Maktoum bin Rashid Al Maktoum, and Sheikh Hamdan bin Rashid Al Maktoum – during a visit to Dubai by Sheikh Zayed bin Sultan Al Nahyan, to attend the wedding of Sheikh Maktoum at his Khawaneej Palace.

Opposite page, below: Sheikh Mohammed in a friendly chat with Sheikh Zayed, about whom His Highness says in his famous book *My Vision – Challenges in the Race for Excellence*: 'Without Sheikh Zayed, Dubai would not have been able to reach its present prominent commercial and economic status. The late Sheikh Zayed unconditionally supported Dubai's development efforts out of his unflinching confidence in the future and the success of the federation. The late Sheikh Zayed never hesitated for one second in supporting any effort to promote the UAE on the world's economic map'.

Previous page: Sheikh Mohammed bin Rashid Al Maktoum was brought up in an environment that cherished strong family ties. His Highness is seen here in a friendly chat with his father Sheikh Rashid bin Saeed Al Maktoum, the founder of modern Dubai.

Sheikh Zayed bin Sultan Al Nahyan and Sheikh Mohammed bin Rashid Al Maktoum share Eid greetings at Sheikh Zayed's Al Baraha Palace in Abu Dhabi. His Highness Sheikh Mohammed describes his relationship with Sheikh Zayed as "one of a father and son".

**ABOVE: A picture expressing true fatherly affection by Sheikh Zayed bin Sultan Al Nahyan attending a camel race. Also seen from right to left, Sheikh Rashid bin Mohammed bin Rashid Al Maktoum, Sheikh Hamdan bin Mohammed bin Rashid Al Maktoum, Sheikh Maktoum bin Mohammed bin Rashid Al Maktoum and Bahrain's Monarch King Hamad bin Isa Al Khalifa.**

**FOLLOWING SPREAD, TOP: The close bond between three of the Al Maktoum brothers is clearly evident in this intimate photograph taken by Noor Ali Rashid at a private luncheon.**

**FOLLOWING SPREAD, BOTTOM: Sheikh Mohammed with Sheikh Maktoum and their younger brother, Sheikh Ahmed bin Rashid Al Maktoum.**

**FOLLOWING SPREAD, RIGHT: One of Noor Ali Rashid's earliest photographs of His Highness Sheikh Mohammed is this charming depiction of him as a boy, lovingly and respectfully looking up to his older brother, Sheikh Maktoum.**

ABOVE: A picture taken many years ago, shows His Highness Sheikh Mohammed bin Rashid Al Maktoum at a horse race with his three eldest sons, from left to right, Sheikh Rashid bin Mohammed bin Rashid Al Maktoum, Sheikh Hamdan bin Mohammed bin Rashid Al Maktoum and Sheikh Maktoum bin Mohammed bin Rashid Al Maktoum.

RIGHT: Sheikh Mohammed in an affectionate hug with his son, Sheikh Maktoum, while attending a horse race.

**ABOVE:** A recent photograph of the three eldest sons of His Highness Sheikh Mohammed bin Rashid Al Maktoum, engaged in a deep discussion. From left to right: Sheikh Hamdan, Sheikh Maktoum and Sheikh Ahmed.

**OPPOSITE PAGE, TOP:** Present and future generations gather at Za'abeel Palace to receive well wishers during Eid. In the front row to the right is His Highness Sheikh Mohammed, Sheikh Hamdan bin Rashid Al Maktoum, and Sheikh Maktoum bin Rashid Al Maktoum. To the left of the picture we see four of Sheikh Mohammed's sons, from left to right, Sheikh Maktoum, Sheikh Rashid, Sheikh Hamdan, and Sheikh Saeed; while to the extreme right is Sheikh Maktoum's oldest son, Sheikh Saeed bin Maktoum bin Rashid Al Maktoum.

**OPPOSITE PAGE, CENTRE:** Sheikh Mohammed at a camel race, accompanied by his sons (from right to left): Sheikh Maktoum, Sheikh Ahmed, Sheikh Saeed, and Sheikh Mansour.

**OPPOSITE PAGE, BOTTOM:** Sheikh Mohammed with three of his sons, from left to right, Sheikh Maktoum, Sheikh Rashid and Sheikh Hamdan. Also seen in the front row is Lieutenant General Dhahi Khalfan Tamim, Director General of Police.

At the Emirates International Endurance Racing, His Highness Sheikh Mohammed is flanked by three of his sons. To his right is His Highness Sheikh Hamdan and His Highness Sheikh Ahmed, and to his left is His Highness Sheikh Majid.

Sheikh Mohammed with some of his children, from left to right: Sheikh Ahmed, Sheikh Rashid, Sheikh Hamdan, Sheikha Maitha, and Sheikh Majid.

Following her winning the karate silver medal at the 15th Asian Olympic Games and describing the close relationship between His Highness Sheikh Mohammed bin Rashid Al Maktoum and his children, Her Highness Sheikha Maitha bint Mohammed bin Rashid Al Maktoum said that her father was her first teacher: "As you know, my father is a true and distinguished sportsman. He always used to advise and direct me, correct my mistakes at the semi and quarter finals . . . . The most important lesson I learned from my father, however, was that one should admit his loss when he fails. This spirit is behind my admission to winning the silver medal instead of the gold." Her Highness explained: "My father used to tell me that he who works hard shall achieve and if he perseveres, he will win in the end. I always remember these words whenever I am participating in a championship anywhere in the world. I also always strive to prepare and be fit enough to achieve victory, which my father always encourages me to do."

RIGHT: The American University of Dubai's graduation ceremony in 2006 took on a personal note for His Highness Sheikh Mohammed when his son, His Highness Sheikh Maktoum, was awarded a Bachelor of Business Administration degree. Cherie Booth QC, who is married to the former British Prime Minister Tony Blair, delivered the keynote address and is also seen in the picture.

BELOW: His Highness Sheikh Tahnoun bin Mohammed Al Nahyan, the Ruler's Representative in the Eastern Region, talking to His Highness Sheikh Mohammed's sons (from left to right) His Highness Sheikh Maktoum bin Mohammed bin Rashid Al Maktoum, the Deputy Ruler of Dubai, His Highness Sheikh Hamdan bin Mohammed bin Rashid Al Maktoum, the Crown Prince of Dubai, and His Highness Sheikh Rashid bin Mohammed bin Rashid Al Maktoum.

OPPOSITE PAGE: His Highness Sheikh Mohammed with his son, His Highness Sheikh Majid bin Mohammed bin Rashid Al Maktoum, during his graduation ceremony from Sandhurst in 2006. Sheikh Majid was presented with the Overseas Sword, awarded to the Overseas Cadet considered by the Sandhurst Commandant to be the best of the intake.

The fatherly affection of His Highness Sheikh Mohammed bin Rashid Al Maktoum is evident through the interaction with his children, his love and caring for them. His Highness is seen in the pictures of this spread, enjoying happy moments with his daughters.

**ABOVE:** His Highness Sheikh Mohammed bin Rashid Al Maktoum spreads cheer among staff and residents at a home for the elderly.

**OPPOSITE PAGE, TOP AND BOTTOM:** Sheikh Mohammed cares greatly about education. His Highness is seen in the top picture on a visit to an elementary school, while he is seen in the bottom picture chatting happily with some of the brighter students.

The pictures in this spread show how keenly His Highness Sheikh Mohammed bin Rashid Al Maktoum follows up on the affairs of all community segments, by constantly communicating with them through field visits to government and semi-government departments and establishments, shopping centres, schools and community associations.

ABOVE: Sheikh Mohammed bin Rashid Al Maktoum chatting with a group of children.

LEFT: A group of girls performing a traditional dance during a festive occasion.

OPPOSITE PAGE: Sheikh Mohammed with a group of young girls during festive celebrations.

# *Chapter 7*

# A man of noble values

His Highness Sheikh Mohammed bin Rashid Al Maktoum truly represents a unique breed of leaders, by successfully combining his monumental official responsibilities, religious duties, family care and personal interests.

One of the most distinguished features of his character is his keenness on extending charity and making people happy in and outside the United Arab Emirates. Sheikh Mohammed is also devoted to helping the needy through generous cash and 'in kind' donations, especially the handicapped rehabilitation and care institutions, orphanages, old age homes and charitable organizations. He is also renowned for launching local, regional and international initiatives to upgrade the standards of education and healthcare services in the Arab world and developing countries.

One of the most important initiatives is the one His Highness unveiled at the World Economic Forum held in Jordan in 2007. It consisted of dedicating a Dhs 37 billion endowment fund to develop a strong knowledge base and nurture a new generation of future leaders in the region's public and private sectors upgrading the standards of scientific research, spreading knowledge, incentivizing a pioneering spirit in businesses, enabling the creative and innovative potential of young generations, updating the concepts of culture and heritage conservation and promoting closer ties between cultures.

This initiative, the largest of its kind in the region, gave a strong momentum to the development of human resources by investing in the development of education and knowledge throughout the Arab world.

The Mohammed Bin Rashid Al Maktoum Foundation, in charge of implementing the initiative, is now managing a wide array of activities and programs, including financing research programs, establishing advanced research centres, schooling grants and subsidizing university research throughout the region. The Foundation also organizes programs for training young leaders in the public and private sectors as well as NGOs, and provides grants and finance to the region's authors and researchers. In his speech announcing this initiative, His Highness emphasized the need to bridge the knowledge gap between the region and the developed world and use all available resources to achieve this goal. He said: "Those in the less than twenty years old age bracket constitute over half of the region's population, and we must develop these human resources using all available means. We have the vision and management capacities needed to educate and prepare these future generations to fully contribute to our development process through this Foundation".

Furthermore, and as part of Sheikh Mohammed's consistent efforts to provide people with a better future, he launched the 'Dubai Cares' initiative, one of the biggest international humanitarian initiatives that focuses on fighting poverty, spreading knowledge and providing education for children in the world's poorest countries. Corporate and individual donations to the initiative in the United Arab Emirates totalled Dhs 1.7 billion, while His Highness matched it with a similar amount, thus raising the total to an unprecedented Dhs 3.4 billion.

On September 3, 2008, His Highness Sheikh Mohammed unveiled 'Noor Dubai' aiming in its first stage at delivering preventative eye care to over one million people in developing countries. The move is part of a drive towards a world free from curable forms of blindness, and a new branch added to the Emirates, flourishing humanitarian tree, shadowing the needy and victims of natural disasters.

In an effort to encourage innovation, His Highness Sheikh Mohammed has announced a wide array of awards both in Dubai and the rest of the UAE, including the Arab Journalism Awards, the Dubai Government Excellence Programme, the Dubai Holy Qu'ran Awards and the Young Business Leaders Awards. These awards have promoted a competitive climate for both the public and private sectors to strive for excellence.

---

LEFT: Sheikh Mohammed and Sheikh Hamdan (second and third from the left) together with Sheikh Zayed and Sheikh Rashid (second and third from the right) perform *Umrah* or 'Lesser Pilgrimage' in Mecca, which is only second to *Hajj*.

## Sheikh Mohammed, the Poet

As for being a formidable and notoriously talented poet, His Highness says that the greatest influences on his development as a poet have been his father, Sheikh Rashid bin Saeed Al Maktoum, and Sheikh Zayed bin Sultan Al Nahyan, who partnered with Sheikh Rashid to become the founding fathers of the UAE. Sheikh Mohammed's schooling period at the Bell Languages School in Cambridge, where he enjoyed a prevailing literary and poetry environment there, also furthered his interest. He began composing Nabati poetry (an ancient form of colloquial Bedouin Arabic) while he was still at school. During his youth, when travelling with Sheikh Rashid; Sheikh Mohammed would often take the poems of some great Arab poets like Al Mutanabbi, Al Buhtouri and Abu Tammam, his favourite classical poets, with him to read on the journey; something which has contributed to his extensive poetic vocabulary.

When Sheikh Mohammed's poems were first published in local newspapers, they appeared under pseudonyms – including Naddawy and Saleet – as he wanted to be sure that people genuinely thought his poetry was good, and that the newspapers were not just publishing his poetry because the author was a member of the ruling family. He received early encouragement from the renowned poetess Fatat Al Arab when she composed a reply to one of his earliest poems – a rare honour for an unknown poet. Nowadays, His Highness is widely acknowledged as one of the finest exponents of Nabati verse, and his works are published under his own name.

He writes about a wide range of topics, from romance idealizing love to current affairs expressing compassion with the grievances of the nation. Wisdom, depicting the contradictions of life and mankind's relationship with the universe, is also one of the most important topics of Sheikh Mohammed's poetry, in addition to the sea and the desert that have always been some of the most important topics inspiring him.

In an effort to spread awareness of his nation's cultural heritage, Sheikh Mohammed has participated in a number of poetic contests with other high-profile poets from the region, including Sheikh Zayed and Sheikh Khalid bin Faisal of Saudi Arabia. These contests involve the poets responding to each other's verses and can be written or oral. Commenting on these contests, Sheikh Mohammed says: "This poetic art is greatly appreciated by people as it arouses the spirit of competition between poets. I support and encourage this art because it brings about communication between poets."

His Highness has also tried to encourage others to compose Nabati verse through his riddles. He composes a poem comprising many questions, unlike the traditional one-line riddle of Western cultures, that people are invited to

RIGHT: At the final ceremony of the Dubai International Holy Qu'ran Awards in 2001. Held during the holy month of Ramadan (Muslim fasting month), the annual awards endeavour to honour those who memorize the Qu'ran and the most prominent Muslim scholars.

BELOW: Seen praying during Eid is Sheikh Mohammed bin Rashid Al Maktoum, and to his left is Sheikh Hamdan bin Rashid Al Maktoum, while to his right are four of his sons (from right), Sheikh Rashid, Sheikh Hamdan, Sheikh Majid and Sheikh Maktoum.

OPPOSITE PAGE TOP AND BOTTOM: Sheikh Mohammed performing *Umrah* at the holy Kaaba. In the image below, His Highness is seen to the extreme left in the company of His Highness Sheikh Hamdan bin Rashid Al Maktoum, Sheikh Rashid and Sheikh Zayed.

FOLLOWING SPREAD: Sheikh Mohammed is immensely popular with all the people of Dubai and the rest of the UAE. Here he takes time to meet a community elder.

attempt to answer. However, they must send their solutions in the form of a Nabati poem that matches the style of Sheikh Mohammed's original. A substantial reward is offered to anyone who manages this feat, and there has been a great response to the riddles from all over the Arab world. There were over 12,000 replies received for the fifth riddle.

## Sheikh Mohammed, the Equestrian

Sheikh Mohammed is renowned for being an accomplished equestrian, who has personally won many awards at endurance races and is one of the world's most prominent owners of horse stables.

Commenting on a question addressed by an Arab journalist about the reason for his interest in horses, His Highness said: "I was astonished when an Arab journalist asked me why I am so interested in horses. I told him horses are not like other animals and bless the households of their owners. They are, furthermore, a source of pride to every Arab and also a symbol of pride and power. God the All Merciful the All Compassionate mentioned horses many times in his holy book, the Qu'ran, and said in one of the verses of the Qu'ran: 'Make ready for them all thou canst of (armed) force and of horses tethered, that thereby ye may dismay the enemy of Allah and your enemy' (Al-Anfal 8:60). And the Prophet (peace and blessings be upon him) said, 'Horses are always the source of good, till the Day of Resurrection' (Reported by Abu Dawood). Whenever I take part in endurance races and encourage my sons and daughters to do likewise, and whenever I enjoy riding and raising horses and encourage my children to do likewise, I am doing something that our fair religion encourages us to do."

"If some people tend to forget that our Arab nation pioneered horsemanship, I don't. We do not just love horses but we also revere and venerate them and consider them a good omen." His Highness explained, adding: "Arabs were the ones who transformed horses' pedigrees into a self sustained science and wrote countless books and poems about horses for well over a millennium. Whenever I think about Arab knights and military leaders, I always visualize them riding their horses. But those glorious great days have long since gone and horses no longer carry knights and leaders. When the sun was setting on pioneering Arab deeds, it started to shine on westerners and their Arab origin horses. It is a known fact that all thoroughbreds in the UK are the descendants of Arab horses, the world's oldest breed . . ." He exclaimed: "Poetry, gallantry, esteem, respect and generosity are some of the most important and enshrined values of Arab chivalry. But although Arab knights disappeared with the passage of time, their horses remained, despite the fact that they were almost on the brink of extinction in some episodes of history. If we leave the economy, technology, pioneering and horses to others, what will be left to us then?"

His Highness went on saying: "Our riders and horses are taking part in international races and winning the most coveted awards and cups in Europe and other major world equestrian centres. I am not claiming that we have completely regained our status regarding horses, but I can say that we are headed in the right direction. Many people are now quite knowledgeable in traditional horse breeding and care methods."

His Highness explained: "Whoever thinks that our interest in breeding and racing horses is purely for economic reasons is wrong, because the love of horses runs in our arteries like blood. I love horses and understand them, but if your understanding of horses is restricted to what your eyes can see, then you don't know much about them. It also means that you will not realize their true beauty until you master the way to deal with them, and then only will you understand why Arabs used to say: Horses know their riders, and did not say that riders know their horses."

Elaborating on his way of dealing with his horses, His Highness said: "When I am with my horses, you see me moving between them, wiping sweat from the bodies of some and feeling the pulse of some others. I also feed them and teach them all the virtues that promote their nobility and gallantry. This kind of relationship is not one-sided, for I also learn from horses and the people around me."

His Highness added: "He who knows how to make horses happy, can also make people happy. He, who knows how to respect horses knows how to appreciate people, and he who knows how to raise the spirit of horses also knows how to promote people's self-confidence. Your caring about horses shall do you good because if you encourage them, they overcome difficulties and lead you to victory. In order to do that, you must know horses closely, care for them and stay beside them if they get sick or face any problems, and most importantly, love them, because they will love you in return."

The victories and championships the Godolphin stables' horses achieved, include the 'Hong Kong', Hong Kong's richest race, won by Fantastic Light in 2000, Moon Ballad in 2003 and Electro Cashinest in 2006.

Despite his great wins, Sheikh Mohammed bin Rashid Al Maktoum very modestly talks about his skills as a tough rider and attributes them to his heritage. In this respect, His Highness says: "It seems that my passion for horses is not personal, but is part of my blood, soul and history."

A dance takes place to the accompaniment of drums. When this photo was taken, the participants were arriving by car rather than the camel of old. A number of the ubiquitous, ex-military Bedford trucks and Land Rovers of the early days of motoring in Dubai can be seen.

Sheikh Mohammed's passion for horses was nurtured from a very young age. Both he and Princess Haya share a remarkable love for horses. Above is a rare photograph of Sheikh Mohammed and Princess Haya riding together during a race.

LEFT: Sheikh Mohammed enjoys a moment at the races with Salem bin Suhail Al Amiri, the first national jockey of the Emirates in the early 1960s.

BELOW: Sheikh Mohammed, riding the dark horse fourth from the left, jockeying for position in one of the first horse races held.

OPPOSITE PAGE: Sheikh Mohammed, an enthusiastic and skilled endurance rider, leaves a dusty trail as he leads a race.

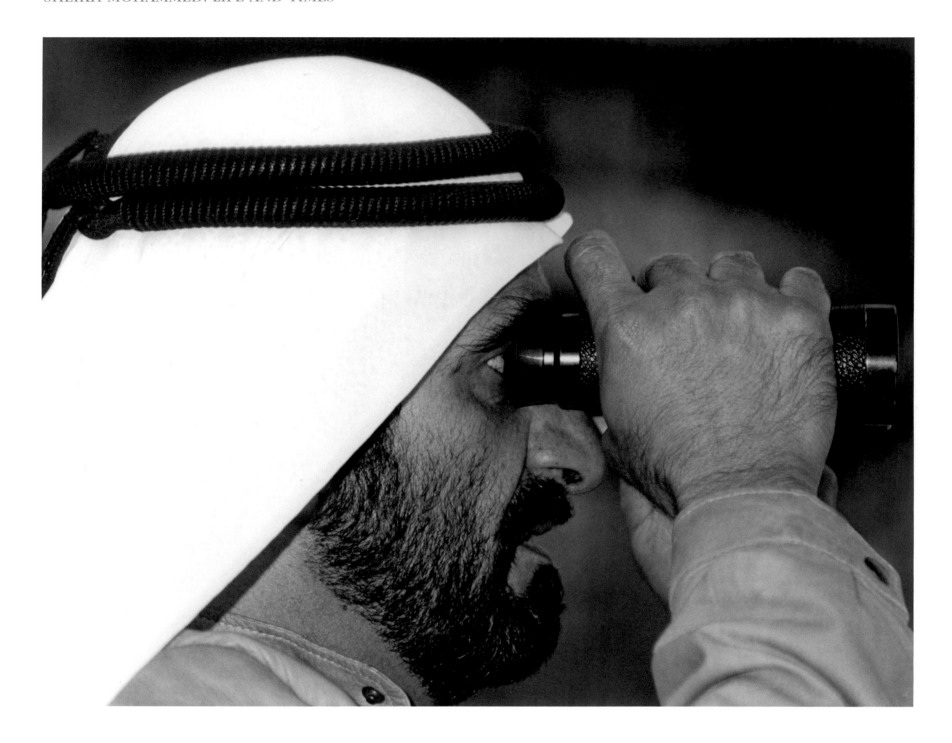

ABOVE: Despite his responsibilities, Sheikh Mohammed still finds time for family matters and equestrian events.

OPPOSITE PAGE, TOP: An enthusiastic rider and one of the world's leading racehorse owners before he died, Sheikh Maktoum is seen holding the trophy for the world's richest horse race, the Dubai World Cup, won in 2003 by his horse, Moon Ballad. Holding the trophy with him is Frankie Dettori, while Sheikh Mohammed and three of his daughters also enjoy the moment.

OPPOSITE PAGE, BOTTOM: First held in 1996, the Dubai World Cup is renowned as the world's richest horse-race. Here, Sheikh Mohammed enjoys a chat with some of the jockeys before the races. The jockey on the right is wearing the colours of the royal stable, Godolphin.

RIGHT: His Highness Sheikh Mohammed and His Highness Sheikh Ahmed bin Saeed Al Maktoum, Chairman of the Dubai Civil Aviation Department, Chairman and Chief Executive of Emirates Airline & Group, during the races at Newmarket in the UK during the 1990s.

OPPOSITE PAGE: Sheikh Mohammed and Princess Haya at the Royal Ascot in 2007. Dubai enjoyed a successful campaign at Ascot that year, with Sheikh Mohammed providing two winners, his brother, Sheikh Hamdan, a third and Godolphin a fourth, while one of Princess Haya's horses achieved second place in one of the major races.

BELOW: Sheikh Mohammed and Princess Haya with Queen Elizabeth II of Great Britain at the Epsom Derby racing festival in 2009.